HOME RUN!
The Year the Records Fell

Compiled from the files of
AP The Associated Press

Sammy Sosa and Mark McGwire (AP/Wide World Photos--Beth A. Keiser)

Sports Publishing Inc.
Champaign, Illinois

www.SportsPublishingInc.com

ACKNOWLEDGMENTS

I want to thank Leslie Krantz of Facts That Matter Inc. for the opportunity and Mike Pearson of Sports Publishing Inc. for his guidance.

This project wouldn't have been possible without the efforts of the sports writers, photographers and freelancers who covered baseball for The Associated Press in 1998.

Special thanks to AP Baseball Writer Ben Walker for his input and to Larry McShane, Barry Wilner, Stephen Wacker and Ira Podell for their help.

A very special thank you to my wife Karen, for her understanding, patience and support.

Paul Montella
September 1998

Mark McGwire shows off the ball he hit for his 62nd home run. (AP/Wide World Photos—Ed Reinke)

©1998 The Associated Press
All rights reserved

Project manager: Michael G. Pearson
Editor: Susan M. McKinney
Book design: Michelle R. Dressen
Book layout: Michelle R. Dressen, Jennifer L. Polson
Dustjacket design: Julie L. Denzer
Coordinating editor: Paul Montella
Production assistant: Vicki Parrillo
Front cover photo: AP/Wide World Photos—
Amy Sancetta
Back cover photo: AP/Wide World Photos—
James A. Finley

ISBN: 1-58261-027-4

Printed in the United States.

SPORTS PUBLISHING INC.
www.SportsPublishingInc.com

TABLE OF CONTENTS

FOREWORD

What a year! The 1998 baseball season has been phenomenal. With Mark McGwire hitting home runs at an unbelievable pace and Sammy Sosa challenging him all the way, the season has been one of tremendous excitement. But more important than even the results have been the class and dignity that these men have shown along with their performances.

My father, Roger Maris, had a real passion for baseball. He felt success was the result of hard work and dedication. He knew what the single-season home run record meant, and it was something he was truly proud of.

My father always tried to instill good values in his children—honor and respect in no matter what it was you were doing. He taught us to be good sports; that if you work hard and try hard, you will be a winner.

Mark McGwire and Sammy Sosa are both winners. My father would have been extremely proud of them, not just for their great seasons but also for their character, heart, and passion for the game. They are outstanding role models for all who watch them play. I know I will always remember what it was like being in the stadium when Mark hit his 61st home run and what it meant to our family when Mark tapped his heart in recognition of our father. To be part of that moment was special.

It was great to be there the following night when Mark hit his record-breaking 62nd home run and then paid tribute to our father in a touching ceremony afterward. Mark said to us, "I held your father's bat that the Hall of Fame had brought with them from Cooperstown earlier in the day and rubbed it against my heart—I knew today would be the day."

I was glad that Sammy Sosa could be there for Mark's record-breaking moment also. It was special for the Maris family to be invited to Chicago and partake in the Sammy Sosa Day Celebration after he hit his 62nd home run as well. Sammy was gracious and personally thanked us for being part of his moment.

In all, 1998 was a great season for baseball and one the Maris family will always remember.

Roger Maris, Jr.

Roger Maris, Jr., right, sits with his brothers, left to right, Randy, Kevin and Rich Maris, as he holds the bat his father, Roger Maris, used to hit his record-setting 61st home run in 1961. (AP/Wide World Photos—Eric Draper)

INTRODUCTION

The harder you try, the tougher it gets. Hitting a home run is one of the most difficult feats in sports.

For 37 years, 61 was a magic number in baseball and one of the most cherished records in sports.

To break Roger Maris' record it would take a special player and the right circumstances.

Entering the 1998 season, many believed the record would fall. The 1990s had become an era of strong, free-swinging hitters, smaller ballparks and expansion; this season, Arizona and Tampa Bay joined the majors.

Babe Ruth hit 60 in 1927. His record held up for 34 years until Maris broke it in 1961, also an expansion year.

Mark McGwire had come the closest with 58 home runs in 1997, which tied for third most in history. The contemporary Paul Bunyan could hit them far and frequent, making him the favorite to hit 62.

Other contenders were Seattle's Ken Griffey Jr. who hit 56 in 1997, Albert Belle of the Chicago White Sox, Juan Gonzalez of Texas, Jeff Bagwell of Houston and Andres Galarraga of Atlanta.

McGwire didn't waste time, hitting four home runs in his first four games, and the great chase was on.

As the season progressed, McGwire became an American hero. He captivated the country and, like Babe Ruth, energized a sport that had fallen on some tough times. He didn't have to endure the hatred and scrutiny that both Hank Aaron and Maris suffered in their quests to break Ruth's career and single-season home run records.

But an unlikely star emerged in Chicago during June. Sammy Sosa of the Cubs hit an amazing 20 home runs that month and officially entered the race.

McGwire vs. Sosa. The 1997 major league home run champion vs. the surprising challenger.

They will be linked forever. Muhammad Ali had Joe Frazier, Affirmed had Alydar and now McGwire had Sosa.

The native of the Dominican Republic, who hit 36 last year, insisted all season that McGwire was The Man and he was just another kid. That didn't stop him from applying the pressure.

Sosa took the lead for 58 minutes on Aug. 19 before McGwire hit his 48th and 49th homers at Chicago. On Sept. 8, he was standing in right field in Busch Stadium when McGwire beat him in the race to 62. On Friday of the final weekend, Sosa hit his 66th homer in Houston and held the lead for about 45 minutes before McGwire answered with his 66th in St. Louis.

McGwire ended the season as mightily as he started it—hitting four homers in the final two days—giving baseball a new magic number: 70. Sosa's season was extended by one day and the Cubs beat the San Francisco Giants in the NL wild-card tiebreaker. He finished with 66.

Both lived by the unwritten code of baseball: The team is everything, and shame to those who take pleasure in personal performance when the team lost.

McGwire had the home run title and Sosa was on his way to the playoffs.

Want to bet McGwire wishes he could change places?

Paul Montella
September 1998

Chicago Cubs slugger Sammy Sosa (AP/Wide World Photos— Beth A. Keiser)

WHAT A SEASON!

By BEN WALKER
AP Baseball Writer

Mark McGwire sent the first signal way back in March.

His grand slam on opening day did more than start the rush to Roger Maris' record. He was telling us, right there and then, that big things were on deck for 1998.

Were they ever.

A home-run race for the ages and a sight to behold: Sammy Sosa running in from right field to embrace McGwire on the night of No. 62.

A startling scene in Baltimore: Cal Ripken on the bench, telling his manager, "I think the time is right" and ending his incomparable streak of 2,632 consecutive games.

Pitching performances that defied all odds: Rookie Kerry Wood striking out 20 in his fifth major league start, David Wells throwing the 13th perfect game in modern history and coming close to another one. Roger Clemens winning 15 in a row.

An expansion year full of hefty numbers, as expected: The New York Yankees winning the most games in AL history (114), one of three clubs that were 100-game winners. And the Florida Marlins taking the worst tumble by a World Series champion.

Heavy hitters galore: A home-run chase that reinvigorated the sport and captivated the nation. Juan Gonzalez and Sosa going for the most RBIs in 60 years, and the first season with more than two players topping 50 homers.

The highest-scoring All-Star game ever.

Huge trades: Mike Piazza going from Los Angeles to Florida to the Mets, Randy Johnson joining Houston. Shakeups at Dodger Stadium,

with Tommy Lasorda in and then out as general manager.

Award races down the final day: Clemens, bidding for his record fifth AL Cy Young, or maybe it'll be Pedro Martinez or Wells. Gonzalez or Mo Vaughn or Nomar Garciaparra or one of the Yankees for the AL MVP. Greg Maddux or Tom Glavine or Kevin Brown for the NL Cy Young.

Plus some positive signs for the future: an increase in attendance and Bud Selig taking the "interim" off his title and turning into a full-time commissioner.

What a season!

In fact, the regular season ended one day after it was supposed to, with the Chicago Cubs beating the San Francisco Giants Sept. 28th in a one-game playoff for the NL wild-card spot.

The Arizona Diamondbacks and Tampa Bay Devil Rays brought something new to baseball, along with a lot of young pitchers and nearly 100 losses each. At Bank One Ballpark, there was a swimming pool beyond the right-center field fence and at Tropicana Field, there was a cigar bar.

While the decimated Marlins stumbled to the worst record in the majors (54 wins,108 losses)—"We stunk," manager Jim Leyland said—the Yankees recovered from an 0-3 start and spent the whole year chasing history.

With Bernie Williams and Derek Jeter dueling for the AL batting title, the Yankees clinched a playoff spot in late August and surpassed the league record of 111 wins, first set by the 1954 Cleveland Indians.

In the home-run race, Maris' 37-year-old mark was passed twice in less than a week.

McGwire set the pace until Sosa hit a record 20 in June. From then on, fans began following the chase game-by-game, at-bat by at-bat.

A quick note to naysayers: Even though this is an expansion season, the overall home-run rate is exactly the same as last year's level.

Along the way, there were other issues. McGwire's use of the muscle-building supplement androstenedione was revealed in an Associated Press story and sparked a national debate, as did an umpire's fan-interference ruling that cost McGwire a 66th home run.

The rivalry between McGwire and Sosa, meanwhile, spawned a friendship that helped unite them and their fans.

Hours before McGwire hit No. 61, he and Sosa sat biceps to biceps at Busch Stadium, praising each other and offering predictions for the future.

"Wouldn't it be great if we just ended up tied?" McGwire said. "I think it would be beautiful."

The next night, McGwire reached the goal that had been demanded of him since the first day of spring training, hitting No. 62. He hugged his son, the Maris family and Sosa in celebration.

At that instant, with fireworks exploding overhead and the whole country cheering, it seemed like baseball had reached its zenith for 1998.

But who knows what's going to happen in October.

Sellout crowds followed Mark McGwire and Sammy Sosa wherever they played, including this scene on September 7 at Busch Stadium in St. Louis when Big Mac hit his 61st home run, tying Roger Maris' record. (AP/World Wide Photos—James A. Finley)

ESTIMATED DISTANCE OF BASEBALL'S LONGEST TAPE MEASURE HOME RUNS

Two of the longest home runs in baseball history were hit in 1998 by Cardinal slugger Mark McGwire. Here's a complete list of the top ten.

- Mickey Mantle, Yankees—1953
  565 feet
  Chuck Stobbs, Senators
  Griffith Stadium

- Babe Ruth, Yankees—1935
  550 feet
  Guy Bush, Pirates
  Forbes Field

- Jimmie Foxx, Red Sox—1936 550 feet
  Sugar Cain, White Sox
  Comiskey Park

- MARK McGWIRE, Cardinals—1998
  545 feet
  Livan Hernandez, Marlins
  Busch Stadium

- MARK McGWIRE, A's—1997
  538 feet
  Randy Johnson, Mariners
  Kingdome

- Willie Stargell, Pirates —1978
  535 feet
  Wayne Twitchell, Expos
  Olympic Stadium

- Dave Kingman, Mets—1976
  530 feet
  Tom Dettore, Cubs
  Wrigley Field

- Andres Galarraga, Rockies—1997
  529 feet
  Kevin Brown, Marlins
  Pro Player

- Ted Williams, Red Sox —1939
  527 feet
  Bob Harris, Tigers
  Tiger Stadium

- MARK McGWIRE, Cardinals —1998
  527 feet
  Paul Wagner, Brewers
  Busch Stadium

NATIONAL LEAGUE 1998 FINAL STANDINGS

EAST DIVISION

	W	L	Pct.	GB
*Atlanta	106	56	.654	—
New York	88	74	.543	18
Philadelphia	75	87	.463	31
Montreal	65	97	.401	41
Florida	54	108	.333	52

CENTRAL DIVISION

	W	L	Pct.	GB
*Houston	102	60	.630	—
*Chicago	89	73	.549	13
St. Louis	83	79	.512	19
Cincinnati	77	85	.475	25
Milwaukee	74	88	.457	28
Pittsburgh	69	93	.426	33

WEST DIVISION

	W	L	Pct.	GB
*San Diego	98	64	.605	—
San Francisco	89	73	.549	9
Los Angeles	83	79	.512	15
Colorado	77	85	.475	21
Arizona	65	97	.401	33

*Playoff qualifier

BATTING LEADERS

Average
Larry Walker, Colorado Rockies, .363

Runs
SAMMY SOSA, Chicago Cubs, 132

RBI
SAMMY SOSA, Chicago Cubs, 158

Hits
Dante Bichette, Colorado Rockies, 219

Doubles
Craig Biggio, Houston Astros, 61

Triples
David Delucci, Arizona Diamondbacks, 12

PITCHING LEADERS

Winning Percentage
John Smoltz, Atlanta Braves, 17-3, .850, 2.90 ERA

Strikeouts
Curt Schilling, Philadelphia Phillies, 300

Saves
Trevor Hoffman, San Diego Padres, 53

Randy Johnson was traded from the Seattle Mariners to the Houston Astros at mid-season and led the Astros to the National League's Central Division title. (AP/Wide World Photos—Gene J. Puskar)

AMERICAN LEAGUE 1998 FINAL STANDINGS

EAST DIVISION

	W	L	Pct.	GB
*New York	114	48	.704	—
*Boston	92	70	.568	22
Toronto	88	74	.543	26
Baltimore	79	83	.488	35
Tampa Bay	63	99	.389	51

CENTRAL DIVISION

	W	L	Pct.	GB
*Cleveland	89	73	.549	—
Chicago	80	82	.494	9
Kansas City	72	89	.447	16+
Minnesota	70	92	.432	19
Detroit	65	97	.401	24

WEST DIVISION

	W	L	Pct.	GB
*Texas	88	74	.543	—
Anaheim	85	77	.525	3
Seattle	76	85	.472	11+
Oakland	74	88	.457	14

* Playoff qualifier

BATTING LEADERS

Average
Bernie Williams, New York Yankees, .339

Runs
Derek Jeter, New York Yankees, 127

RBI
Juan Gonzalez, Texas Rangers, 157

Hits
Alex Rodriguez, Seattle Mariners, 213

Doubles
Juan Gonzalez, Texas Rangers, 50

Triples
Jose Offerman, Kansas City Royals, 13

PITCHING LEADERS

Winning Percentage
(18 decisions)
David Wells, New York Yankees, 18-4, .818, 3.40 ERA

Strikeouts
Roger Clemens, Toronto Blue Jays, 271

Saves
Tom Gordon, Boston Red Sox, 46

New York Yankees pitcher David Wells is carried off the field by his teammates after pitching a perfect game against the Minnesota Twins, May 17, at Yankee Stadium. (AP/Wide World Photos—Lou Requena)

1998 AMERICAN LEAGUE HOME RUN LEADERS

Ken Griffey Jr. Seattle Mariners	56
Albert Belle, Chicago White Sox	49
Jose Canseco, Toronto Blue Jays	46
Juan Gonzalez, Texas Rangers	45
Manny Ramirez, Cleveland Indians	45
Rafael Palmeiro, Baltimore Orioles	43
Alex Rodriguez, Seattle Mariners	42
Mo Vaughn, Boston Red Sox	40
Carlos Delgado, Toronto Blue Jays	38
Shawn Green, Toronto Blue Jays	35
Nomar Garciaparra, Boston Red Sox	35

Seattle's Ken Griffey Jr. led American League sluggers with 56 home runs in 1998. (AP/Wide World Photos—Jay Drowns)

1998 NATIONAL LEAGUE HOME RUN LEADERS

MARK McGWIRE, St. Louis Cardinals	70
SAMMY SOSA, Chicago Cubs	66
Greg Vaughn, San Diego Padres	50
Vinny Castilla, Colorado Rockies	46
Andres Galarraga, Atlanta Braves	44
Moises Alou, Houston Astros	38
Jeremy Burnitz, Milwaukee Brewers	38
Vladimir Guerrero, Montreal Expos	38
Barry Bonds, San Francisco Giants	37
Chipper Jones, Atlanta Braves	34
Javy Lopez, Atlanta Braves	34
Jeff Bagwell, Houston Astros	34

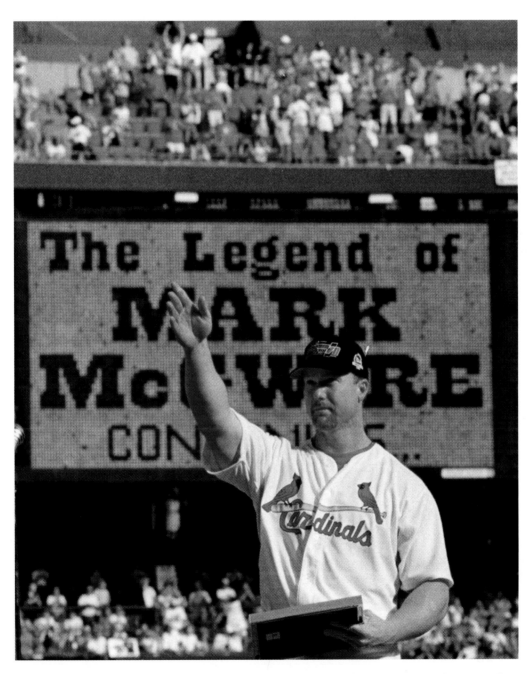

Mark McGwire of the St. Louis Cardinals paced the National League with a record-setting 70 home runs in 1998. (AP/Wide World Photos—James A. Finley)

AUGUST 1, 1997

CARDINALS GRAB BIG MAC

By ROB GLOSTER
AP Sports Writer

"We feel if we get Mark into St. Louis and he sees what a quality baseball environment it is, I think he'll be surprised."
—Walt Jocketty, General Manager, St. Louis Cardinals

OAKLAND, Calif. (AP)—Mark McGwire had to choose between club loyalty and old friendships, between staying with a rebuilding team and going to a possible contender.

He decided it was time to move on for the first time in his career.

"It's not an easy decision to make, but I think you come to a crossroads in your life where change is good for you," said McGwire, baseball's premier power hitter. "I came to that crossroads."

McGwire, one of the last links to the great Oakland teams of the late 1980s, was traded by the Athletics to the St. Louis Cardinals on Thursday for three pitchers after he gave his approval to the deal.

McGwire, who led the majors last season with 52 homers and is among the leaders with 34 this year, has homered with more frequency —once every 12.25 at-bats—than any player in history other than Babe Ruth.

"I don't know how much longer I'm going to play major league baseball," McGwire said. "If I have a chance to help somebody go to the playoffs and World Series, I want to do that now. Oakland is rebuilding and I don't know how much longer it's going to take them."

In return for McGwire, the Athletics got right-handed pitchers T.J. Mathews, Eric Ludwick and Blake Stein. Mathews was the only one of the three in the major leagues at the time of the trade.

The trade will reunite McGwire, 33, with St. Louis manager Tony La Russa, who was with Oakland from 1986-95, and former A's teammates such as Dennis Eckersley, Willie McGee, Rick Honeycutt and Todd Stottlemyre.

The A's feared they wouldn't be able to re-sign McGwire, whose five-year, $28 million contract expires at the end of the season.

St. Louis isn't worried yet about re-signing the first baseman —the third-place Cardinals are more concerned about making up 7$\frac{1}{2}$ games in the NL Central.

Cardinals general manager Walt Jocketty, who spent 14 seasons working in Oakland's front office, called McGwire "a quality bat, an RBI guy in the middle of the lineup, something we've missed this year," and said he thinks the Cardinals have a good chance to keep McGwire beyond this season.

McGwire, whose 363 home runs rank 42nd on baseball's career list, is eligible for free agency at the end of the season. He said he is open to all possibilities, and that playing in the NL for the first time might help him decide where to sign as a free agent after this season.

The Anaheim Angels reportedly are interested in signing McGwire as a free agent, and McGwire has said he would like to live in southern California to be near his 9-year-old son.

SEPTEMBER 16, 1997

McGWIRE SIGNS $28 MILLION DEAL

By R.B. FALLSTROM
AP Sports Writer

ST. LOUIS (AP)—The St. Louis Cardinals have Mark McGwire for at least three more seasons, and they didn't have to tear up the team to keep him.

McGwire, who joined Babe Ruth last week as the only players with consecutive 50-homer seasons, signed a three-year, $28 million deal Tuesday.

The deal includes a $1 million signing bonus and a fourth season at McGwire's option that brings the total package to nearly $40 million.

One of McGwire's agents, Bob Cohen, said the slugger could have commanded at least another million per season on the free-agent market.

Instead, he wanted to stay so much he not only signed for less, he agreed to defer about 25 percent of the money until he retires.

McGwire said he accepted less money to stay with the Cardinals in part because of the response and adulation he's received in St. Louis.

Thousands of fans show up two hours early for games to enjoy McGwire's tape-measure shots in batting practice.

Before joining the Cardinals, McGwire was said to prefer the West Coast because his 9-year-old son lives in southern California with his mother.

Matthew McGwire gave the Cardinals a thumbs-up after a recent visit and had two words for his dad when the deal was announced: "All right!"

"We fully expect him to complete his wonderful career in St. Louis," said Bill DeWitt, head of the Cardinals' ownership group.

"There's a lot of money being passed around, a lot of questions about how much guys are being paid and people looking for the last dollar," general manager Walt Jocketty said. "I can assure you that Mark McGwire did not do that."

The Cardinals had a $44 million payroll without McGwire. They're counting on a healthy increase in season-ticket sales to help bridge the gap.

"We've got a pretty high payroll relative to baseball and relative to a marketplace this size," DeWitt said. "But this city can support it because it's such a great baseball town."

McGwire also is donating $1 million a year to establish a charitable foundation to benefit sexually and physically abused children. McGwire had trouble keeping his composure describing the foundation, pausing for a half-minute at one point. Later, he said he has close friends who were physically and sexually abused.

"Let's just say children have a special place in my heart," McGwire said.

"I just really believe a guy in my position can really help out."

Mark McGwire is overcome by emotion as he talks about his new foundation to aid abused children. (AP/Wide World Photos—Tom Gannon)

OPENING DAY DRAMATICS

By R.B. FALLSTROM
AP Sports Writer

"Opening day, bases loaded, the star, the modern-day Babe Ruth comes up, and hits a grand slam."
— Cardinal teammate Gary Gaetti

ST. LOUIS (AP)—One down, 60 to go.

Mark McGwire started the chase for Roger Maris' record with a dramatic grand slam, leading the St. Louis Cardinals over the Los Angeles Dodgers 6-0.

A sellout crowd of 47,972 screamed in anticipation when Delino DeShields walked on a full count to load the bases with two outs in the fifth inning and McGwire on deck. McGwire didn't disappoint them, hitting a towering drive that cleared the left-field wall and broke open a scoreless game.

"It's an awesome feeling," McGwire said. "How can you not get chills?"

McGwire, who also doubled, overshadowed a strong performance from winner Todd Stottlemyre. The St. Louis starter gave up three hits in seven-plus innings and didn't allow a runner past second base.

McGwire, who hit 58 home runs last season and fell three short of Maris' record, became the first Cardinals player to hit a grand slam on opening day. The shot spoiled Rupert Murdoch's first game as Dodgers owner.

Fans have come to expect such heroics from McGwire after last season, when he hit 24 home runs in 51 games, including one off loser Ramon Martinez, after he was acquired from Oakland on the trading deadline. His 58 tied for third-most in history, and many think he might hit even more in this expansion season.

1

March 31
Cardinals win, 6-0

Vs. Dodgers' Ramon Martinez

At Busch Stadium
St. Louis, Mo.

McGwire is the first Cardinal to hit an grand slam on opening day

388 feet, left field

2

April 2
Cardinals win, 8-5

Vs. Dodgers' Frank Lankford

At Busch Stadium
St. Louis, Mo.

This extra-inning homer is his second game-winner in two contests

368 feet, left field

3

April 3
Cardinals lose, 13-5

Vs. Padres' Mark Langston

At Busch Stadium
St. Louis, Mo.

McGwire ties Graig Nettles at 28th on all-time list with 390th career homer

364 feet, left field

"The energy level here in St. Louis is on another planet," said McGwire after his first home run of 1998

"They can expect whatever they want," McGwire said. "I can only do what I can do."

On the way back to the dugout, he traded exuberant forearm smashes with teammates—almost too exuberant.

"He broke my hand," joked Gary Gaetti, who was on third base when McGwire launched a two-out changeup over the left-field wall to break up a scoreless game. "He was pretty excited."

Nobody was complaining too much.

"I don't know my own strength," McGwire said. "God, I hope I don't hurt anybody. I get a little excited sometimes and I was juiced up at that point."

Mark McGwire started the chase for Roger Maris' single season home run record by hitting a grand slam homer on opening day. (AP/Wide World Photos—Mary Butkus)

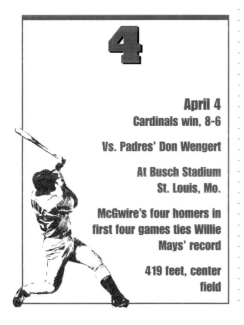

4

April 4
Cardinals win, 8-6

Vs. Padres' Don Wengert

At Busch Stadium
St. Louis, Mo.

McGwire's four homers in first four games ties Willie Mays' record

419 feet, center field

1

April 4
Cubs lose, 3-1

Vs. Expos' Marc Valdes

At Wrigley Field
Chicago, Ill.

The Cubs' home run leader for the past five seasons hits a solo blast

371 feet, right field

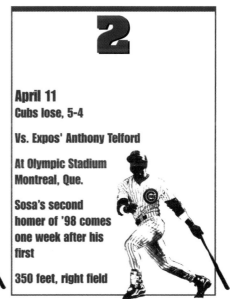

2

April 11
Cubs lose, 5-4

Vs. Expos' Anthony Telford

At Olympic Stadium
Montreal, Que.

Sosa's second homer of '98 comes one week after his first

350 feet, right field

APRIL 14

MAC GETS BACK ON TRACK!

"After being this close to him, I have a lot more fear of him."

—Cardinal teammate Kent Mercker

ST. LOUIS (AP)—Mark McGwire is right back on track.

McGwire hit three home runs, breaking an eight-game homerless drought, as the St. Louis Cardinals routed the Arizona Diamondbacks 15-5.

"I've just been feeling loose at the plate," McGwire said. "It's just a matter of seeing pitches to drive. That's all there is to it."

After tying Willie Mays' major league record by homering in the first four games of the season, McGwire hadn't homered since April 4. He has seven homers—all at Busch Stadium—and 22 RBIs.

However, he's not worrying about his early-season accomplishments or chasing any records.

"You can't think that way," McGwire said. "It's such a long season. Today's over and done with. I'll think about it and enjoy it on the way home, but tomorrow's another day."

McGwire hit a two-run homer in the third, a solo homer in the fifth and added another two-run shot in the eighth with a 462-footer off Barry Manuel. It was his first three-home run game since June 11, 1995, for Oakland against Boston.

However, McGwire admitted this one was special. His son, Matthew, was the Cardinals' bat boy and McGwire was brought out of the Cardinals' dugout after each homer by the 31,477 fans.

"I've had some great exciting games and years in Oakland," McGwire said. "But this is on another level. It's really thrilling."

St. Louis manager Tony La Russa, who managed McGwire for nine seasons in Oakland, has seen it all before.

"I'm always amazed by him," La Russa, said. "I'm not sure if I can come up with any other words to describe him. I'll let you guys who are more creative with words come up with words to describe what a special thing we have here at Busch Stadium."

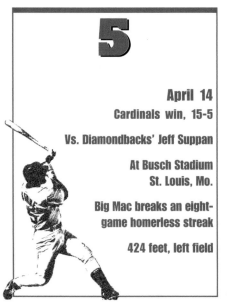

5

April 14

Cardinals win, 15-5

Vs. Diamondbacks' Jeff Suppan

**At Busch Stadium
St. Louis, Mo.**

Big Mac breaks an eight-game homerless streak

424 feet, left field

6

April 14

Cardinals win, 15-5

Vs. Diamondbacks' Jeff Suppan

**At Busch Stadium
St. Louis, Mo.**

One of the season's shortest homers, it regains the lead for St. Louis

347 feet, left field

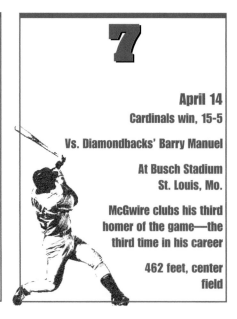

7

April 14

Cardinals win, 15-5

Vs. Diamondbacks' Barry Manuel

**At Busch Stadium
St. Louis, Mo.**

McGwire clubs his third homer of the game—the third time in his career

462 feet, center field

APRIL 14

NO. 1 FAN

ST. LOUIS (AP)—Mark McGwire put on a show for his No. 1 fan.

With his 10-year-old son Matthew serving as the St. Louis Cardinals' bat boy, the first baseman hit three home runs in a game for the third time in his career.

McGwire admits he is glad that his son is getting the opportunity to watch him play.

"The first year I played in the big leagues, I played on the same team as Reggie Jackson," McGwire said. "He told me that he always regretted that he didn't have a child to watch him hit his 500 home runs.

"I just feel fortunate that he is around to see me. That makes it special."

Matthew joined the team on April 11 in San Francisco. But this was the first time that Matthew got to see dad hit one out. McGwire, who averages a home run every 11.9 at-bats, had not homered in his previous eight games before busting out against the Diamondbacks.

Matthew McGwire gives his dad Mark a high-five after McGwire hit his second home run of the night against the Arizona Diamondbacks, April 14, in St. Louis. (AP/Wide World Photos—Harold Jenkins)

BIG MAC GOES TO THE VIDEO

By JOHN F. BONFATTI
AP Sports Writer

Following the game on April 21, Mark McGwire had homered in 27 of the 30 major league parks he'd played in. At that point, he had yet to hit a home run at Philadelphia's Veterans Stadium, Los Angeles' Dodger Stadium or Houston's Astrodome.

PHILADELPHIA (AP)—Chad Blair thinks he knows the biggest secret to Mark McGwire's ability to hit balls long distances.

"What makes him special is his ability to concentrate," said Blair, who is in a good position to judge what makes McGwire the most feared power hitter in the major leagues.

He's the St. Louis Cardinals' video coordinator, a man who McGwire consults after almost every at-bat.

"He takes that concentration into every at-bat," Blair said. "Over 162 games and 600 at-bats, to concentrate that much on every pitch, that's hard to do."

Even though he may be scheduled to have the day off, McGwire still arrives at Veterans Stadium more than five hours before the actual game. One of the first things he does when he gets to the park is check in with Blair.

Unlike some hitters, Blair said McGwire isn't big into studying his own swing. Instead, he said, McGwire spends his video time analyzing pitchers.

First, McGwire has Blair show him the types of pitches the pitchers he'll face throw.

"He'll see the way the guy's ball moves, how his slider moves, the way his sinker moves, does he throw a straight fastball, or is it moving," Blair said.

McGwire said that work helps him build a mental file on each pitcher, and usually gives him an idea of how he thinks a pitcher will pitch him.

"It gives me a better chance every time I get in the box," he said. "It doesn't mean I'm going to get a hit every game. Pitchers are going to get me out—that's a given—but it gives me a better chance and I think that's one of the big reasons why I've come a long way as a hitter."

Blair said McGwire "has got great memory recall on pitchers. He has the ability to remember what a pitcher has done to him.

"He'll come to me after an at-bat to talk about the at-bat," Blair said. "We'll talk about pitches and where they were."

Manager Tony La Russa said McGwire's ability to make adjustments between at-bats is one of the keys to his success. "He's an advance scout's nightmare," he said.

"Somebody will throw a fastball by him, so you tell your club, 'Throw him a fastball,' and he hits a home run," La Russa said. "Or you see him get out on a breaking ball, and you say, 'That's the way to get him out, throw him a breaking ball,' and he hits it out."

McGwire said it's his mental preparation that has him on a historic pace.

"This game is 99 percent mental," he said. "I'm more mentally burned out than I am physically burned out when the season's over, but that's a good thing. It means I've really been using my mind."

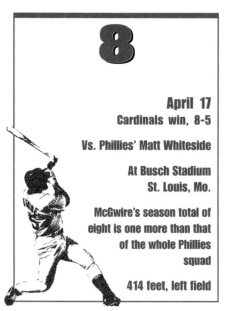

8

April 17
Cardinals win, 8-5

Vs. Phillies' Matt Whiteside

At Busch Stadium St. Louis, Mo.

McGwire's season total of eight is one more than that of the whole Phillies squad

414 feet, left field

9

April 21
Cardinals win, 5-3

Vs. Expos' Trey Moore

At Olympic Stadium Montreal, Que.

Big Mac hits his first homer on the road in 1998

437 feet, left field

BIG MAC LAND

By R.B. FALLSTROM
AP Sports Writer

ST. LOUIS (AP)—Although Mark McGwire has never consumed a Big Mac, he's hit a ball to Big Mac Land.

The St. Louis Cardinals slugger sent a sellout crowd of 47,549 home happy by hitting his major league-leading 21st home run into a section a fast-food restaurant named for him in a 4-3, 12-inning victory over the San Francisco Giants.

Every fan with a ticket gets a free Big Mac sandwich today at McDonald's after McGwire became the first Cardinals player to reach the section, in the upper deck and next to the foul pole in left. Not that McGwire, who's never had a Big Mac, considered it much of a prize.

McDonald's restaurants in St. Louis and the Cardinals unveil Big Mac Land, a theme section in Busch Stadium. The 123-seat area was formerly known as section 363. When a St. Louis player hits a home run into the section, all ticket stubs from that day's game are redeemable the following day for one free Big Mac sandwich. (AP/Wide World Photos—James A. Finley)

3

April 15
Cubs lose, 2-1

Vs. Mets' Dennis Cole

At Shea Stadium
New York, N.Y.

Sammy's only homer in New York City

430 feet, left field

4

April 23
Cubs lose, 4-1

Vs. Padres' Dan Miceli

At Wrigley Field
Chicago, Ill.

Sosa's blast breaks an eight-day homerless drought

420 feet, center field

5

April 24
Cubs lose, 12-4

Vs. Dodgers' Ismael Valdes

At Dodger Stadium
Los Angeles, Calif.

Sammy's second homer of the season against a pitcher named Valdes

430 feet, center field

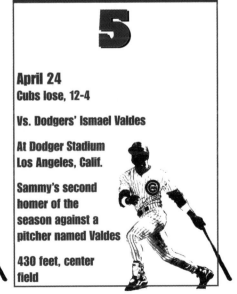

St. Louis Cardinal slugger Mark McGwire celebrates as he runs the bases after one of his record-setting 70 home runs in 1998. (AP/Wide World Photos—Ed Reinke)

Sammy Sosa displays his signature "Home Run Hop," something he did 66 times in 1998 for the Chicago Cubs. (AP/Wide World Photos—Michael S. Green)

APRIL 30

A BLAST INTO THE FOG

By RICK GANO
AP Sports Writer

CHICAGO (AP)—Power pitcher. Power hitter. The 95 mph fastball of rookie Kerry Wood against the prolific home run stroke of Mark McGwire.

"I didn't want to get caught up in that," said Wood, the Chicago Cubs' 20-year-old right-hander. "I have a lot of respect for him, he's just a great hitter. He's always in the back of your mind, but I couldn't put too much emphasis on just McGwire. I had to get the other guys out, too."

Wood did that on a foggy night at Wrigley Field, pitching Chicago to an 8-3 victory over the St. Louis Cardinals with seven strong innings. He struck out McGwire twice, but McGwire later hit his 11th homer, tying him for the major league lead with Vinny Castilla and Ken Griffey Jr.

"He was impressive, just as advertised," Cardinals manager Tony La Russa said of Wood.

The loudest reaction from the crowd all night came when Wood faced McGwire, especially in the first after the first two Cardinals reached base. McGwire then took three straight strikes.

"The respect everybody has for Mark and the young power pitcher, that's interesting to everybody," Cubs manager Jim Riggleman said.

"Mark is the premier power hitter in the game, and any time he comes to the plate, the interest is heightened."

McGwire broke through against reliever Marc Pisciotta in the eighth, hitting a two-run homer through the fog.

"The fog made it interesting between the seventh and eighth innings," said Chicago's Mickey Morandini, who drove in four runs, three with a bases-loaded double in the seventh.

"We couldn't see the scoreboard or the fans. After McGwire hit his homer, it cleared up a little. I'm just glad no one got hurt."

The 9:17 CDT start of the game, delayed 2 hours and 12 minutes by rain, was the latest in Wrigley Field history. During one stretch in the seventh, fog thickened so much the numbers on the center field scoreboard were not readable and outfielders were barely visible.

McGwire was selected as the National League Player of the Month for April.

McGwire hit 10 home runs and drove in 32 runs during the month. He batted .310, scored 20 runs and had a slugging percentage of .738.

Other candidates for April's player award were Chipper Jones of the Atlanta Braves and Mike Piazza of the Los Angeles Dodgers.

10

April 25
Cardinals win , 8-5

Vs. Phillies' Jerry Spradlin

At Veterans Stadium, Philadelphia, Pa.

Two-run homer lifts McGwire's RBI total to 30

419 feet, centerfield

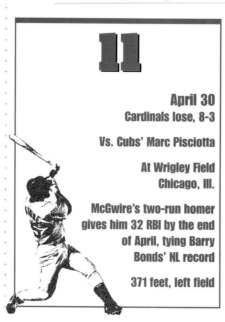

11

April 30
Cardinals lose, 8-3

Vs. Cubs' Marc Pisciotta

At Wrigley Field Chicago, Ill.

McGwire's two-run homer gives him 32 RBI by the end of April, tying Barry Bonds' NL record

371 feet, left field

12

May 1
Cardinals lose, 6-5

Vs. Cubs' Rod Beck

At Wrigley Field Chicago, Ill.

Big Mac's 12th HR gives him 399 career homers, tying him with AlKaline for 26th on all-time list

362 feet, left field

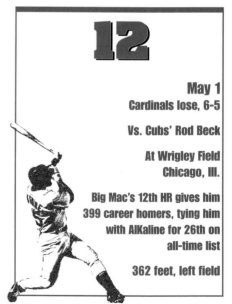

Mark McGwire crosses home plate in front of Chicago Cubs catcher Tyler Houston after hitting a home run out of Wrigley Field. (AP/Wide World Photos—Fred Jewell)

"He's a monster. You can jam him and he'll still hit it out of the park. He's the King Kong of baseball."

— Cubs' Henry Rodriguez on Mark McGwire

6

April 27
Cubs win, 3-1

Vs. Padres' Joey Hamilton

At Qualcomm Stadium
San Diego, Calif.

Sammy's first homer in a Cubs' victory

434 feet, center field

7

May 3
Cubs lose 8-5

Vs. Cardinals' Cliff Politte

At Wrigley Field
Chicago, Ill.

Of Sosa's seven homers, six have come in losing efforts

370 feet, left field

BIG MAC BELTS NO. 400

By RONALD BLUM
AP Sports Writer

McGwire became the first player to reach 400 since Andre Dawson on April 15, 1993. After it bounced into the field-level concourse, McGwire's home run ball was picked up by Harry O'Connell, a 50-year-old from Queens.

"I didn't know it was his 400th home run," he said. Security tracked down O'Connell—who was wearing a Yankees cap—and McGwire gave him an autographed bat for the ball.

Shea Stadium had been just one of two ballparks where McGwire had played without homering. McGwire has connected in 29 of the 30 ballparks he's played in, failing only in Atlanta's Turner Field, where he's appeared in three games.

NEW YORK (AP)—Mark McGwire's 400th home run wasn't much help to the St. Louis Cardinals.

McGwire became the 26th—and fastest—player to reach the milestone, breaking a Babe Ruth record by connecting in the third inning of the Cardinals' 9-2 loss to the New York Mets.

"When people put my name next to Ruth's name, it still blows me away," McGwire said. "I'm still in awe."

McGwire, who hadn't homered in 22 at-bats, walked in the first inning after falling behind 0-2 in the count, his major league-leading 40th of the season.

After Delino DeShields' single in the third, McGwire fell behind 0-2 again against Rick Reed (3-2), then sent a towering fly that sailed just fair of the left-field foul pole, his 13th home run of the season.

"I lost it," McGwire said. "I was looking at the third-base umpire."

McGwire, who put St. Louis ahead 2-1, hit his 400 homers in 4,726 at-bats.

The previous best was 4,854 by Ruth, who finished with a then-record 714. Hank Aaron later extended the record to 755.

McGwire's homer broke a tie with Al Kaline for 26th place on the career list. Next up is Duke Snider at 407, but McGwire's age makes it unlikely he will catch up with Aaron and Ruth.

McGwire, battling injuries, didn't top 140 games played from 1992-96, appearing in just 27 in 1993, 47 in 1994 and 104 in 1995.

"I'm a living example that you can come back from really bad injuries and you can come back from a bad season," McGwire said.

Last year, McGwire, 34, joined Ruth as the only players to homer 50 times in consecutive seasons, hitting 58 following a 52-homer season in 1990. He doesn't think about what his total would be now if he had stayed healthy.

"I've never been a what-if person," he said. "You can't do anything about it. You can't get that time back."

Reed was impressed with the homer, saying it was a fastball that came on a mistake.

"I'm not sure that ball ever came down," he said. "Anywhere you throw it, it's in his power."

New York won its fourth straight and sent the Cardinals to their fourth consecutive loss. St. Louis dropped to 1-7 on a 10-game road trip.

After the game, Cardinals manager Tony La Russa held a short team meeting, then met with several players individually in his office, keeping the clubhouse closed for 30 minutes.

"We're just in a serious funk right now," McGwire said.

On a damp night, La Russa seemed in awe that McGwire was able to put the ball out, getting one of only five hits for St. Louis.

"He continues to do things—home runs in particular—that usually make it all the more impressive," La Russa said.

Mark McGwire watches his 400th career home run sail into the left field stands at Shea Stadium against the New York Mets. Mets catcher Alberto Castillo is at right. (AP/Wide World Photos—Osamu Honda)

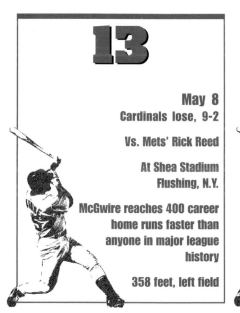

13

May 8
Cardinals lose, 9-2

Vs. Mets' Rick Reed

At Shea Stadium
Flushing, N.Y.

McGwire reaches 400 career home runs faster than anyone in major league history

358 feet, left field

14

May 12
Cardinals win, 6-5

Vs. Brewers' Paul Wagner

At Busch Stadium
St. Louis, Mo.

The upper deck homer is the longest in Busch Stadium history

527 feet, left field

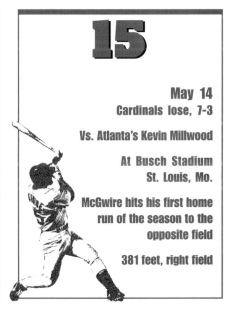

15

May 14
Cardinals lose, 7-3

Vs. Atlanta's Kevin Millwood

At Busch Stadium
St. Louis, Mo.

McGwire hits his first home run of the season to the opposite field

381 feet, right field

MAY 16

McGWIRE DIALS LONG DISTANCE

By R.B. FALLSTROM
AP Sports Writer

"It's the best ball I've ever hit. I don't think I can hit one better than that."
— Mark McGwire on his 545-foot home run vs. the Marlins

ST. LOUIS (AP)—It took Mark McGwire all of four days to top himself.

McGwire hit a drive estimated at a Busch Stadium-record 545 feet, tying for the major league lead with his 16th home run in the Cardinals' 5-4 victory over the Florida Marlins on Saturday night.

The Cardinals' previous record was a drive by McGwire that traveled an estimated 527 feet on May 12. The team has been measuring home runs since 1988.

The estimate also beats McGwire's previous best for distance, a 538-foot homer off Seattle's Randy Johnson June 24, 1997, in the Kingdome when he played for the Oakland Athletics.

"They disappear and get real small, real quick," Marlins manager Jim Leyland said. "It's fortunate they only count as one run."

McGwire tied Colorado's Vinny Castilla for the homer lead with a drive off Livan Hernandez that struck an advertisement below luxury boxes in straightaway center field, leading off the fourth.

The Cardinals, relying on eye-witnesses and reports from the dugout and numerous opinions in the press box, finally estimated the distance in the bottom of the sixth. McGwire wasn't among those consulted.

"I was too worried about the game," McGwire said. "The game is more important than the distance of a home run."

Brian Jordan homered to snap a tie in the bottom of the seventh as the Cardinals broke a three-game losing streak and sent the Marlins to their sixth loss in seven games.

It took the Cardinals about a half-minute to measure Jordan's less impressive 398-foot homer. Jordan connected off Vic Darensbourg.

McGwire's home run started a three-run fourth that included an RBI double by Willie McGee and a run-scoring groundout by John Mabry.

McGWIRE's LONGEST HOME RUNS OF 1998

1. 545 feet at Florida, May 16
2. 527 feet vs. Milwaukee, May 12
3. 511 feet vs. Los Angeles, July 17
4. 509 feet vs. Florida, Aug. 26
5. 501 feet vs. Atlanta, Aug. 30
6. 497 feet at Florida, Sept. 2
7. 485 feet vs. Houston, July 11
8. 478 feet vs. Florida, May 18
9. 477 feet vs. San Francisco, May 23
   477 feet at Pittsburgh, Aug. 22
11. 472 feet vs. Kansas City, June 30
    472 feet at Florida, Sept. 1
13. 471 feet at Philadelphia, May 19

Mark McGwire drops his bat and watches the ball leave the park against the Florida Marlins. Big Mac's 545-foot homer was his longest of 1998. (AP/Wide World Photos—Leon Algee).

16

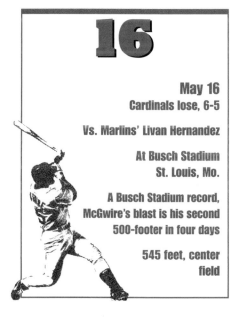

May 16
Cardinals lose, 6-5

Vs. Marlins' Livan Hernandez

At Busch Stadium
St. Louis, Mo.

A Busch Stadium record, McGwire's blast is his second 500-footer in four days

545 feet, center field

8

May 16
Cubs win, 5-4

Vs. Reds' Scott Sullivan

At Cinergy Field
Cincinnati, Ohio

Sosa "goes yard" for the first time in 13 days

420 feet, center field

17

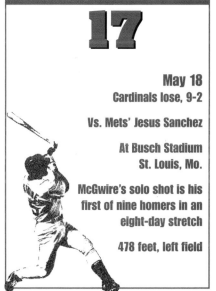

May 18
Cardinals lose, 9-2

Vs. Mets' Jesus Sanchez

At Busch Stadium
St. Louis, Mo.

McGwire's solo shot is his first of nine homers in an eight-day stretch

478 feet, left field

McGWIRE HITS TRIFECTA

By JOHN F. BONFATTI
AP Sports Writer

"If I was sitting in the stands, whether I was a Phillies fan or a Cardinals fan, I'd cheer for a guy who did what he did."
—Phillies pitcher Wayne Gomes, who surrendered McGwire's game-winning homer

PHILADELPHIA (AP)—Mark McGwire obliged those fans who missed his usual batting practice bombardment with a reprise when the home runs really counted.

For the second time this season, the major league home run and RBIs leader hit three homers in a game, including the game-winner in the eighth inning, as the St. Louis Cardinals beat the Philadelphia Phillies 10-8 Tuesday night.

Philadelphia fans responded with a standing ovation when McGwire's third homer in the eighth snapped an 8-8 tie.

"It was an awfully good feeling," McGwire said of the tribute paid by his opponent's fans. "I wish a lot of players could feel what I'm feeling right now."

The players—both his teammates and the Phillies—said McGwire, who has 20 homers in 41 games, deserved the applause.

"Fans like to see offense, and those balls weren't exactly paint-scrapers," Wayne Gomes said. "I'd pay to see a guy who hits like that."

"You don't see a player do things like that," Lou Gant said. "I've never seen a human being hit a ball that far in batting practice or a game."

"He's the most powerful guy I've seen," said the Phillies' Rex Hudler, in his 20th year in pro baseball. "He puts on a show in batting practice that's impressive, then he does it in the game."

Even Cardinals manager Tony La Russa, who has seen all four of McGwire's career three-homer games, shook his head in amazement.

"I'm at a loss for words," he said. "I've got to figure out where this one goes on the list."

It should rank pretty high. The three homers give McGwire 407, tying Duke Snider for 25th on the career list.

The six RBIs tied a career high for McGwire, who leads the NL with 52. He has hit five homers in the last four games. McGwire is now the 12th player to have two three-homer games in a season.

It was the 45th time in his career that McGwire has hit more than one homer in a game. Only nine players in major league history have more multihomer games.

"I'll be very proud of that when I'm done with my career," said the 34-year-old McGwire, who last hit three homers in a game against Arizona on April 14. "But hopefully, I have a lot of years ahead of me."

On a pace to hit 75 homers this year, McGwire dismissed talk that he could break Roger Maris' record of 61 homers in a season.

"When somebody gets to 50 by September, then it's legitimate to talk about," he said. "Right now, I don't think it is."

La Russa said one thing that has gone unnoticed about

McGwire's home runs is that they always seem to come at the right time.

His first homer against the Phillies, a two-run shot that carried 440 feet to dead center in the third, put the Cardinals ahead 3-0. His second, a 471-foot drive which also came with a man aboard, came in the fifth, after the Phillies closed within 3-2 in the fourth.

Then there was the game-winner, a 451-footer, which came after the Phillies had come back to take an 8-7 lead in a game they once trailed 7-2.

"He's been clutch," La Russa said. "I think he's only hit one where the game wasn't close. He keeps hitting them in game situations."

McGwire's third homer of the game made a winner out of John Frascatore (1-2). Juan Acevedo worked the ninth for his second save.

Mark McGwire watches his two-run home run off Philadelphia Phillies' Tyler Green in the fifth inning. (AP/Wide World Photos—George Widman)

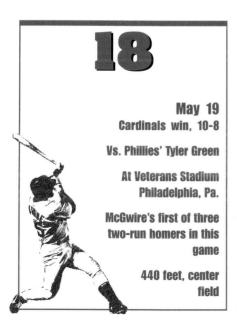

18

May 19
Cardinals win, 10-8

Vs. Phillies' Tyler Green

At Veterans Stadium
Philadelphia, Pa.

McGwire's first of three two-run homers in this game

440 feet, center field

19

May 19
Cardinals win, 10-8

Vs. Phillies' Matt Whiteside

At Veterans Stadium
Philadelphia, Pa.

McGwire's 45th multihomer game of his career

471 feet, left field

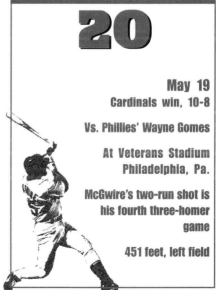

20

May 19
Cardinals win, 10-8

Vs. Phillies' Wayne Gomes

At Veterans Stadium
Philadelphia, Pa.

McGwire's two-run shot is his fourth three-homer game

451 feet, left field

MAY 11

BASEBALL'S MOST FAMOUS BATTING PRACTICE PITCHER

By BEN WALKER
AP Baseball Writer

NEW YORK (AP)—Mark McGwire enjoys picking on certain pitchers, with Orel Hershiser, Mark Langston and Scott Erickson among them.

Then again, when it comes to serving up long balls, none of them is close to Dave McKay.

"I've probably given up more home runs to Mac than anyone else," McKay said.

How many? Try 8,000, McKay estimates.

McKay is the first base coach for the St. Louis Cardinals, and his job includes pitching batting practice. The former major league third baseman held the same job in Oakland for several seasons, meaning he's thrown to McGwire for 10 years.

"It's the best show in baseball," McKay said last week in New York. "He never stops amazing me how far he hits it."

Wherever the Cardinals play these days, crowds come out early to watch baseball's most feared slugger takes his cuts.

The gates at Busch Stadium open 2½ hours before gametime to let fans see their hometown hero.

"A lot of people think he's putting on a show," McKay said.

"But he's not. He's just trying to work on the things he'll do in a game. You can get in a lot of trouble playing home run derby."

Says McGwire: "I never try to air it out."

In fact, it's only been in the last couple of years that McGwire's BP exploits have become a must-see event. And his main setup man thinks he knows why, too.

"When we had the Bash Brothers in Oakland, Jose Canseco liked to put on a show for the fans. He tried to hit them as far as he could," McKay said.

"But Mac used to make me get up close, like 50 feet away, and throw as hard as I could. He wanted to battle you in BP," McKay said. "That meant he wouldn't hit them as far or as often. But he was working on becoming a better hitter."

Nowadays, McGwire prefers that McKay throw him nice, straight and fat pitches from the full 60 feet, 6 inches.

"He likes the ball away a bit, just so he can get into a comfortable rhythm," he said.

McKay knows exactly how he'd pitch McGwire if the matchup were for real.

"I might just walk him," he said.

21

May 22
Cardinals win, 4-3

Vs. Giants' Mark Gardner

At Busch Stadium
St. Louis, Mo.

McGwire passes Duke Snider into 25th place on the all-time home run list.

425 feet, left field

9

May 22
Cubs lose, 8-2

Vs. Braves' Greg Maddux

At Turner Field
Atlanta, Ga.

Sosa tags one against the Braves' three-time Cy Young winner

440 feet, center field

Cardinals batting practice pitcher Dave McKay estimates he's given up nearly 8,000 pre-game home runs to Mark McGwire. (AP/Wide World Photos—Leon Algee)

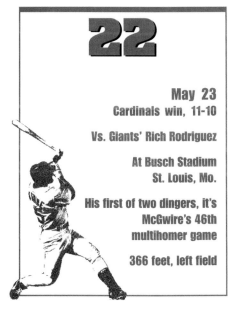

22

May 23
Cardinals win, 11-10

Vs. Giants' Rich Rodriguez

At Busch Stadium
St. Louis, Mo.

His first of two dingers, it's McGwire's 46th multihomer game

366 feet, left field

23

May 23
Cardinals win, 11-10

Vs. Giants' John Johnstone

At Busch Stadium
St. Louis, Mo.

McGwire's 28th home run in 47 games at Busch

477 feet, left field

24

May 24
Cardinals lose, 9-6

Vs. Giants' Robb Nen

At Busch Stadium
St. Louis, Mo.

Big Mac intentionally walked three times before hitting his 12th-inning home run

397 feet, left field

MAY 25

BIG MAC SLAMS 25TH

By R.B. FALLSTROM
AP Sports Writer

ST. LOUIS (AP)—Mark McGwire doesn't put much stock in his ridiculous 83-home run, 202-RBI pace.

The St. Louis Cardinals' slugger became the first player in major league history to hit 25 home runs before June 1 in a 6-1 loss to the Colorado Rockies.

McGwire hit a 2-2 pitch from John Thomson off a Stadium Club window just below Big Mac Land, the section in the upper deck in left field named for him by a fast-food restaurant.

Babe Ruth, Willie Mays, Mickey Mantle and Hank Aaron never had such a start, but that doesn't mean much to McGwire.

"It's great for historians," he said. "I've said that and I'm going to stick to that the rest of my career. Records are no good to you while you're still playing the game.

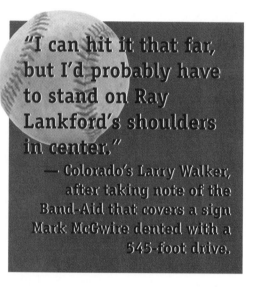

"I can hit it that far, but I'd probably have to stand on Ray Lankford's shoulders in center,"

— Colorado's Larry Walker, after taking note of the Band-Aid that covers a sign Mark McGwire dented with a 545-foot drive.

Period."

It's been a dream start for McGwire, who has nine home runs in his last seven games and four homers in his last three. The latest blast was measured at 433 feet. With five games left in May, he's already tied the Busch Stadium record for homers in a season with 17.

In only the 26th game of the season at Busch Stadium, McGwire tied the stadium record with 17 home runs at home.

McGwire has 30 home runs in 49 career games at Busch. He's also passed Ruth for the best home-run ratio in history. McGwire hits one every 11.60 at-bat and Ruth's ratio was 11.76.

McGwire, who tied Texas' Juan Gonzalez for the major league RBI lead at 61, has 30 homers in 49 games at Busch Stadium since St. Louis acquired him from Oakland last August 31.

25

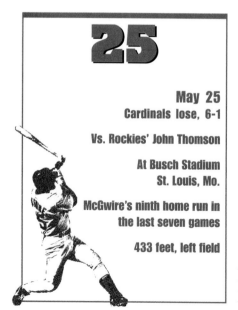

May 25
Cardinals lose, 6-1

Vs. Rockies' John Thomson

At Busch Stadium
St. Louis, Mo.

McGwire's ninth home run in the last seven games

433 feet, left field

10

May 25
Cubs lose, 9-5

Vs. Braves' Kevin Millwood

At Turner Field
Atlanta, Ga.

The first of a 21-homer binge over the next 28 days

410 feet, right field

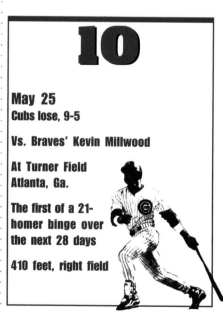

11

May 25
Cubs lose, 9-5

Vs. Braves' Mike Cather

At Turner Field
Atlanta, Ga.

His eighth-inning blast gives Sosa his first multihomer game of 1998

420 feet, center field

MAY 25

CUBS GO DOWN FIGHTING AS SOSA HOMERS TWICE

By TOM SALADINO
AP Sports Writer

ATLANTA (AP)—Atlanta's Kevin Millwood came out on top, even though he wound up on the bottom during a fifth-inning melee.

Millwood won his seventh game and Curtis Pride had a pair of hits and two RBIs before being ejected following a collision at home plate as the Atlanta Braves beat the Chicago Cubs 9-5.

Millwood helped separate Pride and Cubs catcher Sandy Martinez after the two got into a shoving match following the play at the plate.

"I just wanted to get him (Martinez) off of Curtis," Millwood said.

"Obviously nobody wants to be on the bottom of the pile, but I wasn't going to stand around and let the guy hurt Curtis."

Pride, who bruised his right arm in the collision, said he wasn't looking to fight.

"I made a good, hard, clean play. I'm a nice guy and I can't pick a fight," said Pride, who is deaf but does speak.

"I wasn't trying to fight," said Martinez. "He was on top of my head and I wanted to get him off. I pushed him off and he came at me like he wanted to fight."

Millwood left the game with a 6-2 lead, but Sammy Sosa made it close in the eighth with his second homer of the game, a three-run shot off reliever Mike Cather.

The Braves won for the sixth time in seven games and improved to 37-14, their best start in franchise history.

Chicago, which has lost four of its last five, got a run in the fourth on Sosa's 10th homer of the season.

When 1998 eventually concluded, Sammy Sosa had set a major league record for multihomer games in a single season. (AP/ Wide World Photos—Richard Sheinwald)

MAY 27

SOSA SLAMS TWO MORE IN LOSING CAUSE

CHICAGO (AP)—Rico Brogna knows what the Philadelphia Phillies expect from him.

"A first baseman has to be an offensive run producer," said Brogna, who homered, doubled and tied a career-high with five RBIs in leading the Phillies past the Chicago Cubs 10-5.

Sammy Sosa hit two home runs for the Cubs, who lost for the fifth time in six games. He had a solo shot in the eighth inning and a two-run drive, his 13th, in the ninth.

MAY 29

McGWIRE HELPS CARDS BEAT PADRES

By BERNIE WILSON
AP Sports Writer

SAN DIEGO (AP)—Mark McGwire had to wait until the San Diego Padres got into their bullpen before he got a home run.

Padres starter Joey Hamilton, frustrated that his name has come up in trade talks, limited McGwire to a two-run double that broke a scoreless tie in the eighth.

But McGwire hit a two-run homer in the ninth off reliever Dan Miceli as the St. Louis Cardinals scored all their runs in the final two innings to beat the Padres 8-3.

McGwire's major league-leading 26th homer was his first in three games.

McGwire was highly complimentary of Hamilton. "He was very impressive," said McGwire, who tipped his cap to Hamilton after one of his two strikeouts. "He was flat out nasty."

McGwire also hit a bases-loaded double in the eighth, when the Cardinals sent 11 batters to the plate and scored six runs on four hits and four walks.

12

May 27
Cubs lose, 10-5

Vs. Phillies' Darrin Winston

At Wrigley Field
Chicago, Ill.

Sosa's longest home run of the young season

460 feet, left field

13

May 27
Cubs lose, 10-5

Vs. Phillies' Wayne Gomes

At Wrigley Field
Chicago, Ill.

Of Sosa's 13 homers, 11 have come in Cubs losses

400 feet, right field

Mark McGwire: The Big Basher (AP/Wide World Photos—Mary Butkus)

STILL BASHING

When McGwire arrived in St. Louis last July, he brought the forearm bash with him.

A new year brought a new tradition. The 1998 McGwire home run celebration is a high five, followed by an exaggerated punch to the gut directed at the man on deck and selected others.

"It's just something different," McGwire said. "Everybody is doing the same thing now, so we just started hitting our stomachs. That's all."

The punch is supposed to be pulled. Brian Jordan, often the recipient, says McGwire occasionally has gotten a bit too exuberant.

"Sometimes he's caught me off guard," Jordan said. "One time he really got me in the stomach and it was like holy, schmoly. Now I tighten it up."

26

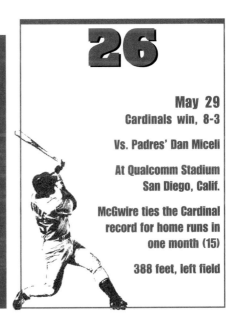

May 29
Cardinals win, 8-3

Vs. Padres' Dan Miceli

At Qualcomm Stadium
San Diego, Calif.

McGwire ties the Cardinal record for home runs in one month (15)

388 feet, left field

McGWIRE LAUNCHES NO. 27

By BERNIE WILSON
AP Sports Writer

> "A guy that strong and the way he's swinging the bat, I mean, he got the best of it. He took advantage of it."
> — Padres' pitcher Andy Ashby on Big Mac's record-tying blast

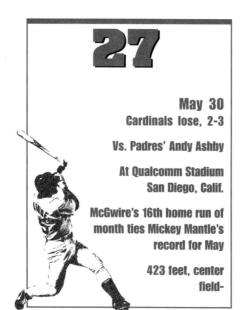

27

May 30

Cardinals lose, 2-3

Vs. Padres' Andy Ashby

**At Qualcomm Stadium
San Diego, Calif.**

McGwire's 16th home run of month ties Mickey Mantle's record for May

423 feet, center field-

SAN DIEGO (AP)—After giving up Mark McGwire's major league-leading 27th home run, Andy Ashby got even with the slugger.

Ashby threw a fat fastball that McGwire launched into the seats in left-center field in the first inning, but the right-hander was careful the rest of the way and the San Diego Padres rallied to beat the St. Louis Cardinals 3-2. Quilvio Veras hit the game-winning single with one out in the ninth.

Ashby tried to throw a fastball up and in on McGwire in the first, but it was simply up and McGwire hit it an estimated 423 feet.

"I didn't know how good I hit it until it was gone," McGwire said.

Ashby walked McGwire in the third and got him to fly out to right in the fifth. He fell behind 3-0 to McGwire leading off the eighth, but threw three sinking fastballs over the outside corner, including a called third strike.

"I wasn't going to lay one in there," Ashby said. "Lord willing, it worked out that way that one didn't come back across the plate. He got me once and I got him once."

McGwire finished 1-for-3 with a walk and is tied with Texas' Juan Gonzalez for the major league RBI lead with 66.

In the ninth, Veras' single off Jeff Brantley (0-1) fell in front of diving right fielder Brian Jordan, scoring Carlos Hernandez with the winning run.

McGwire has already broken the major league record for most home runs by the end of May—Ken Griffey Jr.'s 24 in 1997—and needs just five more to claim the June mark—Griffey's 32 in 1994. Both players chased Roger Maris' record of 61 last year, with McGwire finishing at 58 and Griffey at 56.

Third base coach Rene Lachemann provided a testament to McGwire's power.

Lachemann normally stands well outside the coaching box when the slugger bats, but when McGwire rifled a foul ball toward the seats along the third base line in the first inning, Lachemann moved at least 10 feet farther back.

It was McGwire's 16th homer in May, breaking his own club record for homers in a single month. He had 15 last September. McGwire has 11 homers in as many games, including a two-run shot in Friday night's 8-3 win over the Padres.

St. Louis' Juan Acevedo, moved into the rotation because of injuries, allowed one run and five hits in five innings in his first start since September 29, when he was with the New York Mets.

The crowd of 54,089 was San Diego's third sellout this year.

Big Mac! (AP Photo/Wide World Photos—Joe Cavaretta)

JUNE 1

SAMMY RESUMES LONG-BALL BINGE

CHICAGO (AP)—For the first time all season, Sammy Sosa and Henry Rodriguez homered in the same game. They did it in the same inning off the same pitcher.

"We're not trying to do this every day," Rodriguez said. "We're trying to win ballgames every day."

It will be easier with Sosa back in the lineup. Tonight, he returned with a flourish.

After missing three games with a sprained left thumb, Sosa resumed his long-ball binge with two homers, leading the streaking Chicago Cubs to a 10-2 victory over the Florida Marlins.

"I'm happy to be back and happy to let them know I'm back," said Sosa, who hit a two-run shot in the first and a three-run homer in the eighth, his 14th and 15th homers this year. It was the third time in his last four games that Sosa hit two homers.

"I'm not really 100 percent, but I can hold the bat pretty good,"

Sosa said, his left thumb packed in ice after the game. "When I make contact, it doesn't hurt. When I strike out, it hurts a little. I just forget about it."

The Cubs swept Atlanta over the weekend without Sosa, but could not afford to have him sidelined too long. He is batting .400 (24-for-60) in his last 15 games, with 23 RBI. A career .257 batter, Sosa is hitting .344 overall.

"This year, I'm seeing the ball a lot differently," Sosa said. "I don't try to hit two home runs every at-bat. I'm trying to get a base hit."

Dempster walked Mickey Morandini with one out in the first before Sosa homered. Mark Grace walked and Rodriguez followed with his 12th homer of the season to make it 4-0.

Rodriguez hit an RBI double in the fifth off Kirt Ojala to make it 6-2.

Brant Brown added an RBI single in the sixth.

14

June 1
Cubs win, 10-2

Vs. Marlins' Ryan Dempster

At Wrigley Field Chicago, Ill.

Sosa's first homer in a Cubs victory since May 16

430 feet, left field

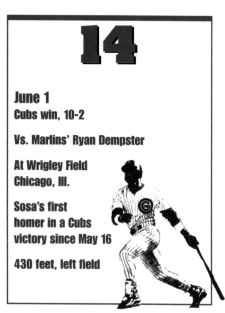

15

June 1
Cubs win, 10-2

Vs. Marlins' Oscar Henriquez

At Wrigley Field Chicago, Ill.

Sammy's 25th career multihomer game

410 feet, center field

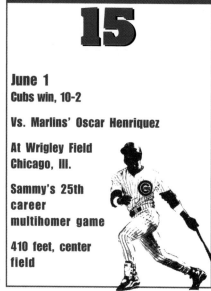

16

June 3
Cubs win, 5-1

Vs. Marlins' Livan Hernandez

At Wrigley Field Chicago, Ill.

Sosa's third homer in three days

370 feet, left field

JUNE 1

McGWIRE STALLED BY BACK SPASMS

By BERNIE WILSON
AP Sports Writer

JUNE 1

BIG MAC PICKED NL PLAYER OF MAY

NEW YORK (AP)—Mark McGwire of the St. Louis Cardinals won his third consecutive NL Player of the Month award.

McGwire, who has spent only four months in the National League, hit 16 home runs and had 32 RBIs in May, giving him a league-leading 27 homers and 68 RBIs on the season. McGwire batted .326 with a .907 slugging percentage and .513 on-base percentage.

Mark Grace of the Chicago Cubs and Greg Vaughn of the San Diego Padres also received consideration for the player award.

SAN DIEGO (AP)—Mark McGwire's run at Roger Maris' home run record has stalled for a few games.

The St. Louis slugger felt lower back spasms while batting in the first inning and was taken out of tonight's 3-2 loss to the San Diego Padres.

McGwire, who leads the major leagues with 27 homers, said he did not expect to play in the Cardinals' three-game series at Los Angeles that begins tonight.

"It's nothing to be concerned about. It probably won't be more than a few games," McGwire said.

He walked off under his own power after hitting a dribbler down the first-base line in the first inning off left-hander Sterling Hitchcock (3-0).

"I took an awkward swing and I felt a twinge," McGwire said. "I know my back like the back of my hand. I'm not going to push it. I've dealt with it every year since '89. I won't miss many games. I've done it worse," he said.

McGwire, who set a big league record for the most home runs through the end of May, leads the NL with 68 RBIs. He is on a pace to shatter Maris' record of 61 home runs set in 1961.

The first baseman has been plagued by injuries throughout his career. He was on the disabled list in 1989 and then every season from 1992-1996 because of problems with his foot, heel, back and ribs.

"I guess that's the biggest obstacle to him in breaking Maris' record is just being able to stay healthy and stay in there," Hitchcock said. "And that's what is going to make it so difficult to break that record."

As for not having to face McGwire more than once, Hitchcock said: "It takes a lot of artillery out of their lineup right there. It was a pretty good break for us."

Hitchcock threw a changeup that broke down and away.

"Obviously after seeing the guys run it up at 95 (mph) over the weekend against him, that changeup had to look like an eephus or something," Hitchcock said. "With the count 3-1, he's geared up anyway."

Mark McGwire is escorted from the field by Cardinals trainer Brad Henderson after suffering lower back spasms when he hit a ground ball in the June 1 game against San Diego. (AP/ Wide World Photos—Joan Fahrenthold)

JUNE 8

SOSA & THE CUBS KEEP ROLLING

By RON LESKO
AP Sports Writer

> "They're not cheering for me, they're cheering for the team. Chicago has a lot of fans all over the world. People love the Cubs."
>
> — Sammy Sosa on the Cubs fans who attended the June 8 game in Minneapolis

17

June 5

Cubs win, 6-5

Vs. White Sox' Jim Parque

At Wrigley Field
Chicago, Ill.

Sosa's homer, his 198th with the Cubs, moved him into a tie with Hank Sauer for seventh place on Chicago's career list.

370 feet, right field

MINNEAPOLIS (AP)—Sammy Sosa homered again, and the home team lost.

Cubs fever hit Minnesota as an animated crowd of 18,077, the largest ever for an interleague game at the dome, watched the Chicago Cubs roll on with an 8-1 victory over the Twins.

It was the 10th straight victory for the lovable losers, who are having their best season of the decade and could be turning into baseball's feel-good hit of the summer.

They certainly sent their boisterous fans home happy Monday, with Sosa tying a team record with a homer in his fifth consecutive game and Jose Hernandez adding a two-run shot.

"It's kind of a good feeling," said starting pitcher Mark Clark (4-6), who got a standing ovation from the fans behind the first-base dugout when he left in the ninth. "I was kind of surprised. I think we've got a lot of Cubs fans up here."

Sosa, clearly the crowd favorite Monday, acknowledged that the team's out-of-the-closet following isn't limited to the Upper Midwest.

Especially when they're playing like this. Chicago's winning streak is its longest since an 11-game surge in 1970.

The Cubs also remained in a first-place tie with Houston in the NL Central, the latest in a season the Cubs have led their division since winning the NL East in 1989.

"Everywhere there are Cubbies fans cheering for us, and more now that we've won 10 in a row and are in first place," said Hernandez, who drove in three runs and has homered in three straight games. "We haven't done that in a long time."

To get their 10th win, the Cubs had to rough up one of their biggest fans in Minnesota: Twins pitcher LaTroy Hawkins, a native of Gary, Indiana.

"I was definitely a Cub fan, Harry Caray all the way," Hawkins said. "But (pitching against the Cubs) wasn't really a big deal."

It was for the Cubs, who scored five runs off Hawkins (3-6) in five-plus innings on seven hits and three walks. That included Sosa's solo homer in the third, a 335-foot, opposite-field shot that barely cleared the right-field wall.

That moved Sosa into a tie with Hack Wilson (1928) and Ryne Sandberg (1989) as the only Cubs to homer in five straight games.

"That's something to be part of," Sosa said. "You get together with those guys up there, they did pretty good for this team when they were playing."

So has Sosa, especially lately. He has a 10-game hitting streak, with a .405 average, 11 homers and 25 RBIs in that span.

Those are power numbers the Twins can only dream about. They've scored just eight runs in their 1-3 start in interleague play.

"They've got good pitching along with good hitting, and that's a tough combination to beat," Matt Lawton said.

Sammy Sosa runs the bases as he watches his third-inning home run off Minnesota pitcher LaTroy Hawkins, June 8. (AP/Wide World Photos—Jim Mone)

28

June 5
Cardinals lose, 3-2

Vs. Giants' Orel Hershiser

At Busch Stadium
St. Louis, Mo.

After missing three games due to back spasms, McGwire hits a homer in his first at bat

409 feet, center field

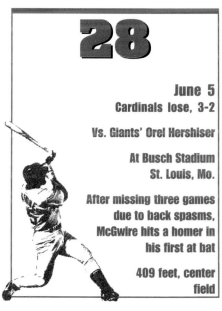

18

June 6
Cubs win, 7-6

Vs. White Sox' Carlos Castillo

At Wrigley Field
Chicago, Ill.

Sosa's June barrage continues as he hits his fifth homer of the month

410 feet, center field

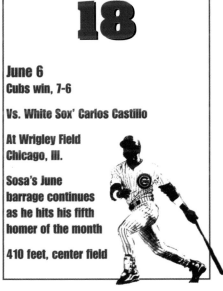

19

June 7
Cubs win, 13-7

Vs. White Sox' James Baldwin

At Wrigley Field
Chicago, Ill.

Third homer in three games for Sammy vs. cross-town rivals

380 feet, center field

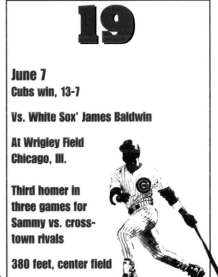

THE PRIDE OF DAMIEN HIGH

By BETH HARRIS
AP Sports Writer

"I've had kids that have had talent, but they're not willing to pay the price. Mark never worried about that."

—Tom Carroll, Mark McGwire's high school coach

LA VERNE, Calif. (AP)—At Damien High, Mark McGwire's choice of a quote accompanying his senior yearbook picture is strangely prophetic in light of his chaotic pursuit of Roger Maris' home run record.

Next to the black-and-white picture of a smiling, freckle-faced McGwire, who graduated from the all-boys Catholic school in 1981, it says: "Life is like a roller coaster with its ups and downs, just sit back and enjoy the ride."

McGwire doesn't always appear to be enjoying his wild ride in the media spotlight. The intensity has reached a fever pitch since he closed within single digits of Maris' record of 61. He had 54 homers going into last night's game against Atlanta.

But that smiling boy, dressed in jacket and tie with a full head of hair, is the person they remember at Damien in this small town 60 miles east of Los Angeles.

The Rev. Patrick Travers taught geometry to McGwire.

"He probably had a little more going for sports than for academics," the principal said, chuckling.

Somewhat shy and well-behaved with a sense of humor is how McGwire's former baseball coach described his star pitcher.

Before McGwire built his reputation as a power-hitting first baseman, he intimidated opposing batters with a 90 mph fastball on the mound behind the high school, with its backdrop of the San Gabriel Mountains. He was 6-foot-5.

"He scared kids because of his size," recalled Tom Carroll, who is now athletic director. "It looked like he was taking the ball and would bring it right to home plate. He's got a long stride. He was working on trying to become a good pitcher."

"I hit, but I didn't care about hitting," McGwire recalled Friday in St. Louis. "I cared about pitching, that's all I wanted to do."

McGwire transferred to Damien from the public high school in Claremont in the middle of his freshman year. He played basketball and baseball for 3½ years, and even had a stint on the golf team when he hurt his shoulder and couldn't pitch during his sophomore year.

"It sounds kind of repetitive and boring, but he worked so hard and he was not afraid to stay and work on his own," said Carroll, who takes no credit for McGwire's skills.

McGwire would perfect his pitching on Sundays and played in a developmental league during the winter.

"All I remember is I did everything myself," he said. "I was self-taught."

As a kid, he played Little League. His father, John, would coach the kids and help prepare the field, according to Carroll.

"Never got any static from Mom and Dad. They were wonderful, very supporting," he said.

But John, a dentist, and Ginger McGwire apparently have different memories of their son's Catholic school days.

"He does not have a good relationship with his old high school," John McGwire said Thursday in Williamsport, Pennsylvania, where he and his wife received an award during the Little League World Series. "He survived it and went on to USC, where he achieved a lot of fame."

McGwire received a scholarship at Southern California, where his teammates included ace pitcher Randy Johnson. He stayed for three years and then played on the 1984

U.S. Olympic team.

While there's no denying the pride Damien staff and students express for the school's most famous graduate, it's hard to find much trace of McGwire other than a photo of him in his old Oakland Athletics uniform propped behind the secretary's desk outside Travers' office.

Visitors have to look hard to find him in the school's modest trophy case.

Behind the smeared glass is the 1980 Baseline League championship trophy with a photo of the baseball team on it. McGwire also

was named baseball MVP in 1981, sharing the honor with Mike Alexander.

Carroll said McGwire hasn't been back to visit since he graduated. Current students would love to see him return for a pep rally, possibly earning them a day off from classes.

"That would be neat," senior Adrian Lozano said. "He could be a good role model being that if you want something so bad you'd go through it. He's had a few up and down games, but he's still going at it."

"I'm hoping he's going to

grace us this year," Travers said. "The kids are beginning to get fired up."

Carroll says it's not necessary for McGwire to give to his alma mater, where the 1,100 students mirror California's diverse population. He believes McGwire's $1 million donation to combat child abuse is enough.

In his mind, Carroll still sees McGwire wiping his face in the dugout between innings. "I still think of him as a kid that went to Damien, just shuffled along through the halls," he said. "He was just a regular kid."

Mark McGwire is in the first row, third from left, in this Damien High School Basketball team photo. (Photo courtesy of Damien High School)

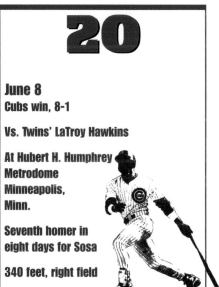

20

June 8
Cubs win, 8-1

Vs. Twins' LaTroy Hawkins

At Hubert H. Humphrey Metrodome Minneapolis, Minn.

Seventh homer in eight days for Sosa

340 feet, right field

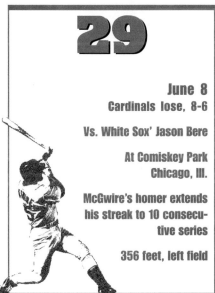

29

June 8
Cardinals lose, 8-6

Vs. White Sox' Jason Bere

At Comiskey Park Chicago, Ill.

McGwire's homer extends his streak to 10 consecutive series

356 feet, left field

30

June 10
Cardinals lose, 10-8

Vs. White Sox's Jim Parque

At Comiskey Park Chicago, Ill.

Only Babe Ruth (1928) hit 30 home runs in a season faster than McGwire

409 feet, center field

HALFWAY HOME

By MEL REISNER
AP Sports Writer

> "The fans got to see what they wanted to see. I didn't see what I wanted to see."
> — Arizona pitcher Andy Benes after surrendering a grand slam home run to Mark McGwire

PHOENIX (AP)—Mark McGwire is halfway home.

McGwire hit his 31st home run in the St. Louis Cardinals' 65th game, a 9-4 victory over the Arizona Diamondbacks. The major league baseball's most glamorous record is 61, set by Roger Maris in 1961, when he had 26 through the New York Yankees' first 65 games.

It was McGwire's only hit, but it came with the bases loaded. The grand slam broke a 1-1 tie and keyed an eight-run third inning that helped the Cardinals win for only the second time in their last nine games.

He declined to talk about his record pace, but did say he was so engrossed in preparing for his second time up against former teammate Andy Benes that he didn't realize the bases were loaded.

"I was into trying to really mentally prepare myself against Andy, because he got me out the first time, so I wasn't aware of who was on base, and I guess maybe it helped me out," said McGwire, who homered in his 11th straight series.

McGwire leads the majors in home runs and is tied with Texas' Juan Gonzalez for the big league lead with 80 RBIs. McGwire has hit 15 home runs in his last 20 games, drawing the admiration of opposing manager Buck Showalter.

"There's something there people want to see," Showalter said.

"It's great for the game, great for the industry, and anyone who feels otherwise is pretty shallow. But you try to face him with nobody on base as much as possible.

McGwire hit seven balls out in batting practice, with one landing on a ledge above the American flag in left-center field and bouncing through a window onto Jefferson Street. Thousands of fans showed up early to watch.

His 438-foot slam and Royce Clayton's three-run homer highlighted the big inning that carried the Cardinals to only their second win in nine games.

31

June 12
Cardinals win, 9-4

Vs. Diamondbacks' Andy Benes

At Bank One Ballpark
Phoenix, Ariz.

McGwire's 11th career grand slam home run

451 feet, left field

21

June 13
Cubs win, 10-8

Vs. Phillies' Mark Portugal

At Veterans Stadium
Philadelphia, Pa.

No. 21 for No. 21

410 feet, right field

Mark McGwire salutes the opponent dugout during batting practice. (AP Photo/Wide World Photos—Mary Butkus)

JUNE 15

SAMMY SCORES A HAT TRICK

"He's the most physically talented player I've ever worked with and I've worked with (Barry) Bonds and (Gary) Sheffield."
— Cubs coach Jeff Pentland on Sammy Sosa

CHICAGO (AP)—Chicago Cubs hitting coach Jeff Pentland has been preaching patience to Sammy Sosa. The advice is paying off.

Sosa's second career three-homer game powered the Cubs to a 6-5 victory against the Milwaukee Brewers.

Sosa hit solo homers off Cal Eldred in the first, third and seventh innings for his 26th career multi-homer game and fourth this year. Fans celebrated Sosa's three-homer game by throwing caps onto the field from the bleachers.

"I'm just trying to go out there and do my job and make contact," said Sosa. "The more patient you are up there, the more you can hit."

Sosa has 32 walks this season after getting only 45 all last season and is batting .335 after coming into the season with a .257 average.

The Cubs broke a 5-all tie in the eighth on one-out singles by Jose Hernandez and Scott Servais off Doug Jones (3-3). Manny Alexander followed with a sacrifice fly to left, to score Hernandez and give the Cubs their second win in their last six games.

Sosa hit his first homer and 22nd of the year with two out in the first, sending a 1-0 pitch into the right field seats.

After the Brewers took a 2-1 lead in the second on Valentin's two-run homer, the Cubs went back ahead in the bottom of the inning on an RBI double by Alexander and an RBI single by Wood.

Sosa connected again with one out in the third, a towering shot onto Waveland Avenue behind the left field bleachers. His third homer was another moon shot, again landing over the left field bleachers to make it 5-2.

"Every time we'd try to make an adjustment against Sosa, he'd counter us," Milwaukee catcher Bobby Hughes said. "It was very frustrating."

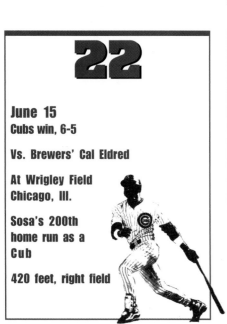

22

June 15
Cubs win, 6-5

Vs. Brewers' Cal Eldred

At Wrigley Field
Chicago, Ill.

Sosa's 200th home run as a Cub

420 feet, right field

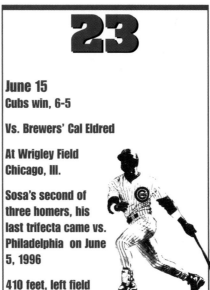

23

June 15
Cubs win, 6-5

Vs. Brewers' Cal Eldred

At Wrigley Field
Chicago, Ill.

Sosa's second of three homers, his last trifecta came vs. Philadelphia on June 5, 1996

410 feet, left field

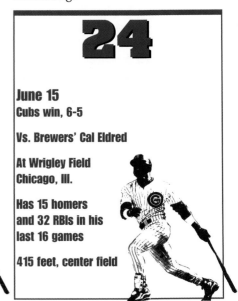

24

June 15
Cubs win, 6-5

Vs. Brewers' Cal Eldred

At Wrigley Field
Chicago, Ill.

Has 15 homers and 32 RBIs in his last 16 games

415 feet, center field

Sammy Sosa is congratulated by third base coach Tom Gamboa (39) after hitting his second homer of the night in the third inning against the Milwaukee Brewers, June 15, in Chicago. He had three home runs in the Cubs' 6-5 victory. (AP/Wide World Photos—Fred Jewell)

On June 15, Sosa became the 28th Cub to hit three in a game. He has hit home runs in 15 of his last 16 games.

32

June 17
Cardinals lose, 5-6

Vs. Astros' Jose Lima

At Astrodome
Houston, Tex.

Big Mac's first home run in the Astrodome

347 feet, left field

25

June 17
Cubs lose, 6-5

Vs. Brewers' Bronswell Patrick

At Wrigley Field
Chicago, Ill.

Sosa's first home run in a Cubs loss since May 27

430 feet, left field

JUNE 18

McGWIRE GOES "RAINBOW"

By MICHAEL A. LUTZ
AP Sports Writer

With his homer vs. Houston on June 18, McGwire moved further ahead of the pace set by Roger Maris in 1961. McGwire has 33 homers in St. Louis' first 70 games—Maris had 27 in the New York Yankees' first 70 games.

HOUSTON (AP)—Everyone but the Houston Astros went home happy.

A record crowd delighted at Mark McGwire's record-setting 449-foot homer as the St. Louis Cardinals held off the Houston Astros for a 7-6 victory.

"This was three outstanding games for us," McGwire said. "This is what baseball is all about. I just want to play baseball. I play this game for one reason, to win, that's all I do."

McGwire's 33rd home run sailed into the rainbow upper deck and set the major league record for most homers hit through June, breaking the mark previously set by Ken Griffey Jr. in 1994. McGwire still has 11 games this month to add to the record.

McGwire's homer came before the largest crowd of the three-game series, 43,806. A three-game total of 115,775 set a record for a three-game series with the Cardinals.

McGwire did have plenty of help in beating the Astros.

Ron Gant drove in three runs to help the Cardinals to an early 5-2 lead. Ray Lankford and McGwire hit back-to-back homers in the fifth inning that chased Shane Reynolds (7-5), who lost for the first time in four home decisions.

Lankford led off the fifth with his eighth homer and McGwire followed with his shot into the Astrodome's rainbow deck.

Big Mac tosses his bat and watches his 33rd home run fly into the Astrodome's upper deck, June 18th, in Houston. (AP/Wide World Photos—Pat Sullivan)

HOME RUN KING? THAT'S JOE BAUMAN!

By BEN WALKER
AP Baseball Writer

33

June 18
Cardinals win, 7-6

Vs. Astros' Shane Reynolds

At Astrodome
Houston, Tex.

McGwire hits only the 11th
upper-deck homer in
Astrodome history

449 feet, left field

Joe Bauman was expecting the call, sort of.

Because when it comes time to talk about hitting home runs—a whole lot of home runs, that is—Bauman is the guy to ask. He hit 72 in 1954 for the Roswell Rockets of the Class C Longhorn League, a pro mark that still stands.

Mark McGwire? Sammy Sosa? Not even close, at least not yet.

"But it wouldn't offend me if they got my record," Bauman said from his home in Roswell, N.M. "They can get it just like I got it.

"It's really something what McGwire and Sosa have done. I've been following it," he said. "It's rekindled interest in baseball after that strike a few years ago and the World Series debacle."

Bauman had hit 50 and 53 home runs the previous two years in the Longhorn League when Roswell bought his contract for 1954. At 32, and having gotten only one at-bat as high as Triple-A, he was near the end of his career.

Yet the 6-foot-5, left-handed first baseman decided the monthly salary of $600 could help supplement the money he would make running a gas station in Roswell. What followed was one of the most monstrous seasons by a hitter ever.

Along with his 72 home runs, Bauman hit .400, had 224 RBIs, scored 188 runs and walked 150 times, all in just 138 games.

The fence in right field was a more-than-fair 330 feet. His only benefit was the high altitude, helping the ball carry.

Bauman went into a final day doubleheader at Artesia, N.M., with 69 home runs, tying the pro record set twice in the minors.

"I could feel the pressure building," recalled Bauman, now retired at age 76. "I wanted to get that record right away."

Bauman did it, homering on his first at-bat in the opener. He hit two more home runs in the second game, not that he did any celebrating on the field.

"Back then, you just got around the bases in a reasonable time," he said. "Nothing special."

The crowd took note, though. As was the custom in the Longhorn League, the next-to-lowest rung in the six levels of minors, fans stuck dollar bills in the chicken-wire backstop. That day, it was reported, about $800 was left for him to collect.

Bauman hit 46 homers for Roswell in 1955 and retired during the 1956 season. Like a lot of ballplayers with big numbers in the minors those days, he never got a shot in the bigs.

In later years, he worked at his gas station and ran a tire distributorship in the New Mexico town fabled for a UFO sighting.

The 72 flying objects he hit in 1954, however, always created a stir.

"On the minor league circuit out there, he was an absolute phenomenon," remembered U.S. Sen. Pete Domenici of New Mexico. "We all heard about him and how he smacked 'em."

Domenici said he never got to pitch to Bauman. In 1954, the future politician was a wild right-hander in the minors, playing for Albuquerque in the West Texas-New Mexico League.

"He was the legend," Domenici said. "There was a lot of talk about why he never made it to the majors."

Nowadays, Bauman is content to follow the exploits of McGwire and Sosa from afar, watching on television when he can.

"I think it'll go down to the wire with them to see who gets the most," he said. "If they both stay healthy, I'd say they could each hit four more."

Which would leave them short of Bauman's mark.

"Oh, I did it a long time ago, and it was in the minor leagues," he said. "But it's still a record."

JUNE 19

SAMMY CONNECTS TWICE, BUT CUBS LOSE

By RICK GANO
AP Sports Writer

CHICAGO (AP)—With the Chicago Cubs sending homers flying out of Wrigley Field once again, the Philadelphia Phillies resorted to some old-fashioned hustle to win the game.

"The winds were blowing out in a gale," Phillies manager Terry Francona said after Mike Lieberthal's 12th-inning sacrifice fly gave his team a 9-8 victory over the homer-happy Cubs.

Sosa hit two more homers, giving him 27 for the season, 18 in his last 20 games and 14 in June, matching Ryne Sandberg's club record from 1990. He is tied with Ken Griffey Jr. for second in the majors behind Mark McGwire.

Sosa is one homer shy of the June record for homers, held by four people, including Roger Maris and Babe Ruth.

"I don't know anything about that record. I'm just trying to make contact. I'm just going up there knowing what I want to do, having an idea and not swinging at bad pitches. We just have to win some games. My goal is to win the division."

Chicago's Brant Brown, who hit three homers yesterday, tied the game with a two-run shot in the bottom of the ninth off Mark Leiter. The Cubs have 14 homers in their last five games and both Brown and Sosa are on a tear. But Chicago has dropped seven of its last 10 games.

"Sammy has carried us to another level, given us a chance to win but we're having trouble holding the other club down," Cubs manager Jim Riggleman said.

Sosa's second homer of the game tied the game 5-5 in the fifth off Carlton Loewer.

Sosa homered in the first for a 1-0 lead. Abreu's double tied the game in the second but the Cubs went ahead 2-1 in the bottom half on consecutive doubles by Hernandez and Jeff Blauser.

26

June 19
Cubs lose, 9-8

Vs. Phillies' Carlton Loewer

At Wrigley Field
Chicago, Ill.

Two homers shy of the major league record for June, held by four players

380 feet, left field

27

June 19
Cubs lose, 9-8

Vs. Phillies' Carlton Loewer

At Wrigley Field
Chicago, Ill.

Sosa's 27th multihomer game of his career, including his fifth this season.

378 feet, left field

Slammin' Sammy Sosa prepares to connect with the ball during a game against the Philadelphia Phillies, June 18. Sosa has hit 16 homers in his last 18 games. (AP/Wide World Photos—Fred Jewell)

JUNE 20

SAMMY CONNECTS FOR TWO . . . AGAIN!

"I've heard announcers talk about balls going onto Waveland, but they might have to go to another street."
— Phillies manager Terry Francona after Sammy Sosa's 500-foot home run

CHICAGO (AP)—Sammy Sosa insists he's no Mark McGwire. He just hits home runs like him.

Sosa hit two homers for the second straight day and set a major league record with 16 home runs in June, leading Kerry Wood and the Chicago Cubs past the Philadelphia Phillies 9-4.

"I've never seen anything like it. The game of baseball hasn't seen anything like it," teammate Mark Grace said of Sosa's hot streak. Wood (7-3), who turned 21 last Tuesday, hit his first big league home run and struck out 11 in 7 1-3 innings.

Sosa had a two-run homer in the third and hit a towering three-run blast in the sixth that landed on the roof deck of a building across Waveland Avenue behind the left-field bleachers.

"He was just trying to show me up," Wood said, laughing, about Sosa's second shot. "I enjoy every home run Sammy hits."

So does Sosa, who now has 20 home runs and 40 RBIs in his last 21 games, and 29 homers for the season.

Sosa, who hit two yesterday against the Phillies and three on June 15 against Milwaukee, has 28 career multihomer games.

The second homer, off Toby Borland, was McGwire-like in its height and distance. It was officially registered at a modest 440 feet.

"I've seen a lot of home runs here but that's the farthest I've ever seen one go," Grace said. "No human being can keep up this hot streak."

"It was one of the hardest hit balls I've ever seen," Borland said.

Babe Ruth (1930), Bob Johnson (1934), Roger Maris (1961) and Pedro Guerrero (1985) also had hit 15 home runs in June. The major league record for most home runs in any month is 18, set by Detroit's Rudy York in August 1937.

The Cubs have nine games left in June.

The sellout crowd of 39,761, the second largest of the season, tried to get Wood to come out of the dugout for a curtain call, chanting his name, but he refused. Sosa obliged the crowd after his second homer.

And how would Wood pitch to Sosa?

"I'd walk him," Wood said.

28

June 20
Cubs win, 9-4

Vs. Phillies' Matt Beech

At Wrigley Field
Chicago, Ill.

Sosa's 19th home run in 21 games

366 feet, left field

29

June 20
Cubs win, 9-4

Vs. Phillies' Toby Borland

At Wrigley Field
Chicago, Ill.

Sammy hits one on top of a roof ACROSS Waveland Avenue

500 feet, left field

Sammy Sosa is greeted by teammate Mark Grace after he hit a home run in the fourth inning of the Phillies game June 21. (AP/Wide World Photos—Mike Fisher)

30

June 21
Cubs lose, 7-2

Vs. Phillies' Tyler Green

At Wrigley Field
Chicago, Ill.

Sammy's fifth
home run in three
days

380 feet, right field

31

June 24
Cubs lose, 7-6

Vs. Tigers' Seth Greisinger

At Tiger Stadium
Detroit, Mich.

Sosa's 18th home
run of June ties
Rudy York's 61-year-
old record for most
homers in a month

390 feet, left field

34

June 24
Cardinals lose, 14-3

Vs. Indians' Jaret Wright

At Jacobs Field
Cleveland, Ohio

McGwire's eighth homer at
Jacobs Field sets a record
for visiting players

433 feet, left field

JUNE 25

McGWIRE CROWNED "KING OF THE JAKE"

By KEN BERGER
AP Sports Writer

"If there's one guy in baseball who we want to do it, it's him."
—Cleveland's Jim Thome on Mark McGwire's attempt to break Roger Maris' home run record of 61

CLEVELAND (AP)—He is the undisputed king of the Jake. With swings like thunderclaps, Mark McGwire bounces balls off his favorite scoreboard as if playing a game of squash in the land of the giants.

Steel beams, concrete steps and jumbotrons are under serious assault, and they're losing.

McGwire hit his 35th homer, nearly becoming the first player to hit a ball out of Jacobs Field, but the Indians got two homers from Jim Thome to beat the St. Louis Cardinals 8-2.

A night after homering in a 14-3 loss to the Indians, McGwire's attack on the 5-year-old stadium again went for naught. Asked to talk about it, he said, "No. We lost."

His 461-foot homer off Dave Burba would have left the stadium if it hadn't collided with a steel beam on the left-field scoreboard. Everyone was admiring it—except McGwire.

"I just don't like losing," McGwire said. "I'm sort of disappointed in the way it went here."

Thome, a good friend of McGwire's who sent the slugger a 12-pack of beer after the first game of the series, talked more about McGwire's power than his own.

"It's truly a pleasure to watch him, to watch how he handles himself," said Thome. "He's such a gentleman."

McGwire has 35 homers in 71 games, missing six of the Cardinals'

first 77. In 1961, Maris had 31 homers through 77 games and didn't hit his 35th until game No. 86.

"I've always thought that of all the people I've seen, his chances of doing it are the best," Indians manager Mike Hargrove said. "Not only is he big and strong, but I think mentally he can handle it."

McGwire hit a 2-2 curveball from Burba (9-5) with two outs in the first, giving the Cardinals a 1-0 lead. It was the second-longest homer hit at the ballpark. McGwire, the only player to reach the left-field scoreboard, owns the top three.

Though colossal, McGwire's 461-foot homer wasn't even worthy of his top 10, which is led by a 545-foot bionic blast at Busch Stadium earlier this season.

The longest of his nine homers at Jacobs Field—tops among visiting players—was a 485-foot shot off Orel Hershiser that dented a beer advertisement on the scoreboard last April 30.

"I felt sorry for Burba," Cleveland shortstop Omar Vizquel said.

"But I enjoyed this one as much as Hershiser's. It's amazing to see a ball travel that far."

All that kept it from leaving the ballpark was the steel beam between the left-field foul pole and the scoreboard behind the bleachers. A couple of inches to the left or right, and it would have reached the parking garage across the street.

"I thought it was foul," said Burba, who gave up McGwire's 55th

Big Mac signs autographs before the game against the Cleveland Indians at Jacobs Field in Cleveland. (AP/Wide World Photos—Tony Dejak)

homer last September 24. "I looked in for a new ball and Sandy was just staring. I never saw the ball. Apparently, it went pretty far."

Thome hit a two-run homer in the fifth, his 21st, then made it 5-2 with a solo shot off Bobby Witt in the eighth. The first homer, coming after David Justice singled, traveled 394 feet—puny by McGwire standards. But Thome's eighth-inning blast, estimated at 436 feet, sailed over trees and a wall guarding the center-field picnic area.

"Thome is an outstanding player. One of the best," McGwire said.

"It blows my mind some of the things he does with the bat."

Burba allowed two runs and six hits in 7 2-3 innings, becoming Cleveland's first nine-game winner. He was lifted when McGwire came up after Delino DeShields singled with two outs in the eighth. Paul Shuey got McGwire to line out to Vizquel, who was nearly knocked over by the liner.

"Burba said, 'I'm not scared of McGwire,'" Hargrove said. "I said, 'Me neither. Let's have Shuey face him.'"

35

June 25
Cardinals lose, 8-2

Vs. Indians' Dave Burba

At Jacobs Field
Cleveland, Ohio

In the Cardinals' 77th game, McGwire tied the mark for most homers by a St. Louis player since Jack Clark hit 35 in 1987.

461 feet, left field

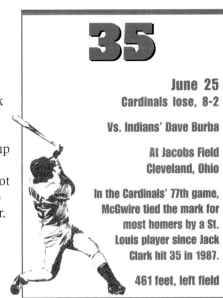

JUNE 25

SOSA BREAKS RECORD IN YORK'S HOMETOWN STADIUM

DETROIT (AP)—Sammy Sosa is proud of the records he's set lately.

He doesn't, however, want to become the story of the Chicago Cubs' season at the expense of his team.

Sosa broke the major league record for homers in a month tonight.

But Tony Clark's three-run homer was the decisive hit as the Detroit Tigers beat the Cubs 6-4.

Sosa hit his 32nd homer leading off the seventh inning. It was his 19th home run in June, breaking the major league mark of 18 set by Detroit's Rudy York in August 1937. Sosa broke the NL record of 17 set by San Francisco's Willie Mays in August 1965 on Tuesday night.

"I'm still thinking about the game. It would've been much better if we'd have won," Sosa said.

Sosa has connected 12 times in his last 13 games, and 23 times with 45 RBIs in the last 26 games.

The crowd of 30,688 fans, second-largest of the season in Tiger Stadium, demanded—and got—a curtain call after Sosa's homer.

"I've never seen a curtain call on the road," Cubs manager Jim Riggleman said, "but we had support from a lot of our fans, and there are some great Detroit fans."

Even the Tigers didn't dispute that Sosa and Chicago starter Kerry Wood were the big reasons for the big crowd. But they hope the win draws people back.

"To have this kind of feeling in our own ballpark with all these people was great," manager Buddy Bell said after the Tigers' third straight win.

Clark's homer, an estimated 450-foot blast to dead center field off Terry Mulholland, broke a 3-3 tie and gave the Tigers a two-game sweep of the Cubs, who have lost five straight and 12 of 16.

Detroit's Damion Easley homered and Geronimo Berroa, making his Tigers debut, hit a two-run double off Wood.

Henry Rodriguez homered for the fourth straight game and Mickey Morandini also hit a home run for the Cubs.

> "I'm happy I'm in the book, but for me it don't mean nothing right now because we lost the game."
> — Sammy Sosa, after hitting his record 19th home run in June

32

June 25
Cubs lose, 6-4

Vs. Tigers' Brian Moehler

At Tiger Stadium
Detroit, Mich.

Sosa connects for the 12th time in his last 13 games

400 feet, right field

NO JUNE SWOON FOR SAMMY

A list of Sammy Sosa's 20 record-setting home runs in June, 1998:

1. June 1 vs. Florida, 430 feet
2. June 1 vs. Florida, 410 feet
3. June 3 vs. Florida, 370 feet
4. June 5 vs. Chicago White Sox, 370 feet
5. June 6 vs. Chicago White Sox, 410 feet
6. June 7 vs. Chicago White Sox, 380 feet
7. June 8 at Minnesota, 340 feet
8. June 13 at Philadelphia, 410 feet
9. June 15 vs. Milwaukee, 420 feet
10. June 15 vs. Milwaukee, 410 feet
11. June 15 vs. Milwaukee, 415 feet
12. June 17 vs. Milwaukee, 430 feet
13. June 19 vs. Philadelphia, 380 feet
14. June 19 vs. Philadelphia, 378 feet
15. June 20 vs. Philadelphia, 366 feet
16. June 20 vs. Philadelphia, 500 feet
17. June 21 vs. Philadelphia, 380 feet
18. June 24 at Detroit, 390 feet
19. June 25 at Detroit, 400 feet
20. June 30 vs. Arizona, 364 feet

Sammy Sosa, right, rounds the bases past Detroit Tigers shortstop Deivi Cruz after hitting a solo home run in the seventh inning to break the major-league record of home runs in a month, June 25, in Detroit. It was Sosa's 19th homer of the month. (AP/Wide World Photos—Richard Sheinwald)

JUNE 26

POWERBALL!

By DOUG TUCKER
AP Sports Writer

KANSAS CITY, Mo. (AP)— One of Kauffman Stadium's biggest crowds of the season showed up early on Friday to watch Sammy Sosa take batting practice.

They were treated to quite a show.

One day after erasing the major league record for home runs in a month, the Chicago Cubs outfielder crushed one pitch nearly 450 feet to near the base of the scoreboard in dead center. Another carried almost that far over the left-field fence and a third splashed into the water display in left-center. Each clout drew gasps and applause.

"If I keep hitting home runs, maybe people will like me even more," the grinning Sosa said before the Cubs took infield practice for their interleague game against the Kansas City Royals. "I feel like I'm just lucky to be in the right place at the right time."

Sosa said he'd never heard of Rudy York before his leadoff shot in the seventh Thursday night at Detroit. It was Sosa's 19th homer in June, breaking York's record for homers in a month set in August 1937 for the Detroit Tigers.

With four more games remaining in June and Sosa riding the hottest power streak of his life, the record may not sit on 19 for very long.

"I never was thinking of setting the record," said Sosa, who had 32 homers altogether and 12 in his last 13 games going into Friday night.

"But I'm in pretty good shape right now and I'm a lot more disciplined at the plate."

While he'd never heard of Rudy York, Sosa does know all about Mark McGwire, the powerful St. Louis first baseman who hit his 35th home run in Cleveland Thursday night about the same time Sosa was hitting his 32nd. Both, all of a sudden, are on pace to challenge Roger Maris' record of 61 homers in a season.

"Mark McGwire is in a different world. He's my idol. He's the man," Sosa said.

While he can't keep people from charting his progress toward the Maris record, Sosa would hate for anyone to think that he's competing against McGwire for attention and glory.

"No matter what people say, he's still my idol. I have a lot of respect for that guy," he said.

"He's the guy everybody is looking for. I'm not going to go crazy. I'm not going to get over-anxious. I'm just going to keep the plan I have right now. I have to stay patient and thank God for giving me so much opportunity. I have to continue to be the best player I can be."

Tony Muser, Sosa's hitting coach last year before the Royals hired him at the All-Star break as their manager, is not surprised at what his old charge has done.

"He's had periods throughout his career when he would get extremely hot. There were times you couldn't get him out," Muser said. "He could hit any pitch at any time out of the ballpark."

As Sosa's former hitting coach, Muser might be expected to have a better idea than most how to pitch to him.

"We do have a battle plan on how to approach Sammy these next three games," Muser said. "But our pitchers have to carry out that battle plan. If we don't do that, Sammy may put some balls in the parking lot."

> "I'm just one of those lucky guys who's there at the right time. I just want to keep doing my job."
> — Sammy Sosa

Sammy Sosa waves to the crowd after hitting a solo home run in the eighth inning against the Arizona Diamondbacks, June 30, in Chicago. The homer extended Sosa's own major league record for most home runs in a month. (AP/Wide World Photos—Fred Jewell)

36

June 27
Cardinals win, 7-2

Vs. Twins' Mike Trombley

At Hubert H. Humphrey Metrodome
Minneapolis, Minn.

Most single-season homers by a Cardinal since Stan Musial's 36 in 1949

431 feet, left field

37

June 30
Cardinals lose, 6-1

Vs. Royals' Glendon Rusch

At Busch Stadium
St. Louis, Mo.

McGwire ties Reggie Jackson for most home runs ever before the All-Star break

472 feet, left field

33

June 30
Cubs lose, 5-4

Vs. Diamondbacks' Alan Embree

At Wrigley Field
Chicago, Ill.

His 20th and final home run of June

364 feet, left field

JUNE 18

SOSA'S KEY WORD: PATIENCE

By NANCY ARMOUR
AP Sports Writer

"To be a complete player, you have to do everything. Since Opening Day, I said to myself, I have to go out and try to make contact. Don't swing at so many bad pitches, because that was my problem before."

— Sammy Sosa

CHICAGO (AP)—Sammy Sosa no longer feels he must hit a home run or do something big to spark the Chicago Cubs' offense.

He has learned to be patient. And now that he's not worried about crushing the ball, he's hitting better than ever.

"The old Sammy's philosophy was get up there and take three swings. It didn't matter if they were strikes or balls," said Jeff Pentland, Chicago's hitting coach. "He feels like there are better hitters around him, so there's no sense of urgency to hold up the whole ball club."

Sosa has homered 16 times in his last 19 games, including three in one game Monday against Milwaukee. He was 0-for-4 last night with one walk.

Sosa hit his 25th home run on June 17, tying him with Andres Galarraga of Atlanta for second-best in the National League and third in the majors. Mark McGwire of St. Louis hit his 33rd last night; Seattle's Ken Griffey Jr. has 26.

Sosa has always been known as a power hitter, a guy who could crush the ball as well as anyone in the majors. But he had a problem with consistency. One week he'd carry a ball club, the next he couldn't hit the ball.

He's the Cubs' only 30-30 player—he's hit 30-plus homers and stolen 30-plus bases in a season twice—and one of only eight to hit 40 or more home runs in a season. But he also holds Chicago's record for strikeouts, fanning 174 times last year.

When the Cubs were struggling through last year's dismal season, Sosa took a lot of criticism as a selfish, flashy player.

At the end of the season, Pentland sat down with Sosa and to him his only problem was impatience. He wasn't waiting for the right pitch. Pentland gave Sosa tapes of other players to watch, and Sosa worked on it during the winter while he was back home in the Dominican Republic.

"Last year I was in a situation where I was swinging at every pitch," Sosa said. "This year I have a different attitude."

Of course, it helps that Sosa has other hitters behind him. With the addition of players like Jeff Blauser, Matt Mieske, Mickey Morandini and Henry Rodriguez—Sosa's buddy from the Dominican Republic—the pressure is no longer just on Sosa and Mark Grace.

"Now I can see everything, I'm more relaxed and I can go to right field," Sosa said. "And we're winning. That takes the pressure off of anyone."

Sosa is batting .333, second only to Grace, and he's driven in 64 runs. He's averaging a home run every 10.56 at-bats and is on track to hit 58 home runs, something not even Hack Wilson or Ernie Banks could do.

"I don't like to say I'm red hot. I know myself that I'm playing good. I just have to contribute everything to win the game and just keep doing what I'm doing," Sosa said. "Maybe after the year I can say I was red hot."

Until then, the Cubs and their fans will just sit back and watch Sosa's show. And what a show it is, Pentland said.

"It's just so much fun to watch him," Pentland said. "It's not supposed to be that easy."

Sammy Sosa warms up by the on-deck circle. (AP/Wide World Photos—David J. Phillip)

THE GREATEST SHOW IN BASEBALL

By BEN WALKER
AP Baseball Writer

> "I'll tell you, he feels more pressure in BP than in the game. I know on days when we cancel BP and just hit inside in the cage, he's got a smile on his face."
> — Cardinals manager Tony La Russa on Mark McGwire

HOUSTON (AP)—The Greatest Show in Baseball—Mark McGwire's power display in batting practice—may not be coming to a stadium near you.

Growing weary of the pregame circus, McGwire says he might cut back on taking BP in the future.

"It's totally out of hand," he said before the St. Louis Cardinals played Houston on Thursday night. "I feel like a caged animal."

A few hours later, McGwire hit his major league-leading 33rd home run, putting him on a pace to shatter Roger Maris' record of 61 homers in 1961. And wherever McGwire plays, the crowds come out early to watch him warm up.

In Phoenix last weekend, his swings were shown on the scoreboard and the distance of his drives were posted. McGwire added to his lore by hitting a ball completely out of the Bank One Ballpark.

In Houston this week, about 15,000 fans packed the left-center field stands two hours in advance and even Astros manager Larry Dierker stuck around to watch. A couple of TV crews filmed BP from the seats, and a much larger than usual media contingent at the Astrodome surrounded McGwire.

"I didn't like it," McGwire said. "It made me very uncomfortable."

As a result, "I'm thinking seriously about not taking batting practice some days," he said.

Cardinals manager Tony La Russa said he and McGwire talked about the situation Wednesday.

"I know if you asked him, he'd rather take BP at 3 in the afternoon when no one's around," La Russa said.

"I mean, we're in the entertainment business and it's great entertainment to see him do what he does," he said. "But on the other hand, the idea of batting practice is to get ready to play the game. And you have to do that the way you feel comfortable. It's just a matter of priorities."

La Russa, by the way, made batting practice optional on Thursday.

McGwire took part and drew a standing ovation for three shots into the rainbow deck at the Astrodome.

In two days, by the way, McGwire hit a total of six BP drives into the top deck at the 'Dome. Only nine balls had been hit there in regular-season games in the ballpark's 34-year history—that is, until McGwire did it in the fifth inning against Houston starter Shane Reynolds.

McGwire broke the June record for homers of 32 set by Ken Griffey Jr. in 1994. The Cardinals still have 11 more games left in the month.

The crowd of 43,806—which helped Houston set an attendance record for a weekday three-game series—gave McGwire a standing ovation as he rounded the bases after his 449-foot drive to left field.

McGwire moved further ahead of the pace set by Maris in 1961.

*St. Louis Cardinals slugger Mark McGwire prepares for his turn in the batting cage.
(AP/Wide World Photos—Ron Frehm)*

McGwire has 33 home runs in St. Louis' first 70 games; Maris had 27 in the New York Yankees' first 70 games.

Fans, though, are sure to be disappointed if they don't see him.

Earlier this season, the Philadelphia Phillies got several angry letters and phone calls after McGwire sat out a game at Veterans Stadium.

La Russa wants to make sure McGwire conserves his energy, especially as the summer heats up. That means the first baseman may not take batting practice prior to day games that follow night games.

"There's no doubt in my mind he won't take BP Sunday" at home before the game against Arizona, La Russa said.

As to where and when McGwire might also skip his pre-game swings, there's no telling.

"Everywhere we go, the media writes that, 'The show is coming to town,'" McGwire said. "It's ridiculous."

JUNE 27

THE McGWIRE RULES

By HAL BOCK
AP Sports Writer

SOSA: NL PLAYER OF THE MONTH FOR JUNE

NEW YORK (AP)—Sammy Sosa of the Chicago Cubs made the National League player of the month choice for June easy by hitting a record 20 home runs last month.

Besides his 20 homers, Sosa drove in 40 runs, scored 25 and had a slugging average of .842.

Other candidates were Gary Sheffield of Los Angeles and Jeff Bagwell of Houston for the player award.

Introducing Mark McGwire, baseball's newest recluse.

McGwire has decided, with the endorsement of the St. Louis Cardinals, that media ground rules are necessary as he pursues one of the most glamorous single-season records in sports— 61 home runs. The man has muscles on his muscles. He wants rules, give him rules. He'll get no argument here.

So from now on, anybody who wants to hear what McGwire thinks about The Home Run Chase will have to do it on a rigid schedule.

On the road, McGwire will do an informal interview for about a half-hour beginning 3½ hours before the first game of each series. Media types who show up on the second or third day of the series will be out of luck.

At home, there will be no formal pregame access and any interview requests must be set up in advance.

Now, let's see who is in the appointment book today. Maybe the Cardinals should give out numbers like they do in department stores for kids waiting to see Santa Claus at Christmas time. No appointment. No interview. Rules are rules.

McGwire, of course, will also be available after games to discuss the game and nothing but the game. Not Roger Maris, not The Chase. Just that day's game.

There will be no telephone or live-shot TV interviews because too many people want to do them and the man has only so much time.

The restrictions went into effect shortly after McGwire passed the halfway point on the road to Maris. Are the rules a sign of pressure setting in? Maris, remember, facing a much smaller media mob, lost patches of hair as his season and chase progressed.

This, though, is only June. If MacZilla is getting squeamish now, wait until August when blast furnace temperatures start heating up The Chase.

Wait until recalcitrant pitchers decide to stop challenging him and give him nothing to hit. Wait until then.

By then, McGwire will be the Greta Garbo of sluggers. Expect him to show up one day wearing sun glasses, hiding under a floppy hat and demanding to be alone.

Particularly galling for him has been the fuss created by batting practice when he tees off on coach Dave McKay, who has given up, oh, 15,000 or so batting practice homers to the big guy over the years. Every-

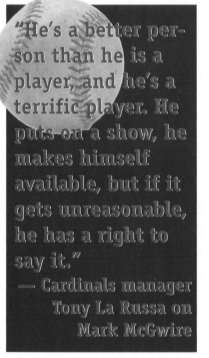

"He's a better person than he is a player, and he's a terrific player. He puts on a show, he makes himself available, but if it gets unreasonable, he has a right to say it."
— Cardinals manager Tony La Russa on Mark McGwire

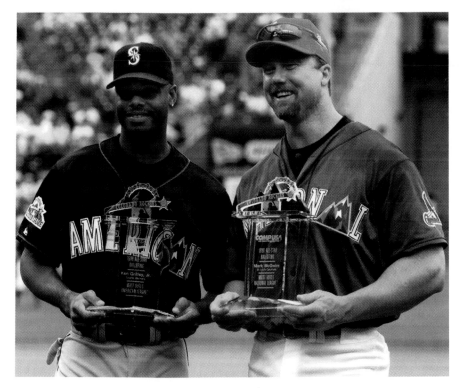

Ken Griffey Jr., left, and Mark McGwire were presented trophies, July 6, for being the top vote-getters in the 69th All-Star game. (AP/Wide World Photos—Beth A. Keiser)

JUNE 29

BIG MAC PACES ALL-STAR VOTING

By BEN WALKER
AP Baseball Writer

NEW YORK (AP)—All those home runs made Mark McGwire a shoo-in to start in the All-Star game. All Sammy Sosa can hope for, however, is a chance to be a backup.

McGwire, leading the majors with 36 homers, was the top vote-getter in NL results with 3,377,145 votes. He was the fans' choice to start for the sixth time overall, the first five coming when he played for Oakland.

"I think it's going to be great," the St. Louis slugger said over the weekend. "It's been great that I've been able to play in the All-Star game so many years for the American League, and now I get to do it for the National League."

But Sosa, whose 19 home runs in June set a major league record for most homers in any month, has to hope he's picked as a reserve for next Tuesday night's game at Coors Field at Denver.

The Chicago Cubs star, who has hit 32 homers, finished sixth among outfielders and was only 12th overall in the fan voting.

thing stops when McGwire steps in. Fans, media, other players are all riveted to the show.

This, McGwire has decided, is a bad thing. He feels cornered by all the attention. So now, batting practice is not a given for him. McGwire says he will skip it sometimes. And fans who come for the show can watch Royce Clayton or Delino DeShields swing instead of Big Mac.

All of this, the Cardinals say, is necessary because of the fuss McGwire's moon-shot home runs have caused. The condition is exacerbated by the frequency with which he hits them. This gets people excited and causes questions to be asked of a man who wants nothing more than a little peace and quiet.

No one could have been surprised by this turn of events. McGwire finished last season with 58 home runs, becoming the first hitter since Babe Ruth to have consecutive 50-plus homer seasons. His remarkable ability to hit home runs is why the Cardinals gave him a $28.5 million contract for three years.

Manager Tony La Russa, noting the frenzy surrounding McGwire, is sympathetic to the plight of his slugger.

La Russa, of course, can relate only marginally to McGwire's problem since he never hit a major league home run, never coming closer than a couple of triples that were seven years apart. He batted .199 and never needed rules to hold off the media blitz.

Here's a friendly suggestion for McGwire.

Pack a lunch pail every morning and become a plumber. The pay isn't quite as good but at least nobody bothers them while they're working.

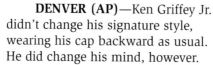
JULY 6

THE HOME RUN DERBY AT COORS

By TOM WITHERS
AP Sports Writer

DENVER (AP)—Ken Griffey Jr. didn't change his signature style, wearing his cap backward as usual. He did change his mind, however.

Griffey, who less than an hour before the All-Star Home Run Derby began was still insisting he would skip this year's competition, won the glamour event by beating Cleveland's Jim Thome in the final.

Griffey reversed his decision after being booed by a Coors Field record crowd of 51,231 while accepting a trophy for being the All-Star game's top vote-getter, named on more than 4.2 million ballots.

"I don't like to get booed. I don't think anybody does," said Griffey, who hit 19 homers in the three rounds and beat Thome 3-2 in the final round. "This is not a time to get booed, the All-Star game. If they want to see me do the home run competition, the fans, there were 4 million reasons why I did it."

As for Mark McGwire, his performance was a surprise, too.

Baseball's home-run leader managed just four home runs and failed to get past the first round. McGwire came to Denver with 37 homers, and many figured if he didn't win the title, he would certainly test the laws of gravity 5,280 feet above sea level.

But except for a 510-foot shot to dead center—the longest of the day—McGwire looked more like a singles hitter than the game's most feared hitter.

"I like the ball middle in, and the pitches were middle away," McGwire said. "So, sorry everybody."

Thome, who choked last year in front of the hometown fans at Jacobs Field by failing to hit one homer, hit eight in both the first and second rounds.

"This was great just to be in it," he said. "I hope they ask me back."

Early Monday afternoon, Griffey was insisting he would pass up the chance to rocket balls through the thin Colorado air. He reluctantly entered last year's event in Cleveland despite getting just a few hours rest after the Mariners played a late Sunday night game.

With his Seattle Mariners cap turned around, Griffey dug into the dirt as his name was announced to loud boos.

"I figured there would be a few, but not like that," he said.

But when he was introduced as the final AL entrant, he received a warm ovation, and by the time he walked to the plate for his first round, many in the crowd were standing.

After connecting eight times to advance, he slowly walked back to the AL dugout, tipped his cap to the fans and hugged his 4-year-old son, Trey.

Then it was McGwire's turn. He hit two weak grounders before driving one over the wall in

Seattle's Ken Griffey Jr. watches his hit in the final round of the Home Run Derby at Coors Field in Denver, July 6. Griffey won the event with 19 homers in three rounds. (AP/ Wide World Photos—David Zalubowski)

straightaway center, hitting a sign just below the Rockpile section of seats. The announced estimated distance of 510 feet surpassed the unofficial stadium record, a 496-foot shot hit by Mike Piazza last year.

Thome, Baltimore's Rafael Palmeiro, Colorado's Vinny Castilla and Houston's Moises Alou all finished the first round with seven homers, but Alou was eliminated because he has less regular-season homers than the others.

Atlanta's Javy Lopez and

Seattle's Alex Rodriguez had five homers each. Detroit's Damian Easley led off the event and managed just two homers, one more than the Braves' Chipper Jones.

Before Monday's workouts, McGwire, who along with Griffey and the Cubs' Sammy Sosa, will spend the second half chasing Roger Maris' record of 61 homers in a season, said he still can't believe he's mentioned along with some of the game's great long-ball hitters.

"It still blows me away, it re-

ally does," he said. "Considering that when I was a kid, all I wanted to do was pitch. It wasn't until my sophomore year in college that I turned into a hitter, never knowing I'd get a chance to go to the big leagues.

"The next thing you know, they're talking about my name along with Babe Ruth, Maris, Mantle down the line. It's overwhelming. I don't think it will really hit me until I'm retired."

ROGER'S RACE WITH THE BABE

By JIM DONAGHY
AP Baseball Writer

Watching from the box seats when Mark McGwire hit No. 62 were the sons and daughters of Roger Maris. McGwire climbed into the stands to hug them and share the moment their father couldn't.

"I wanted to embrace him for what he did and kind of share in the moment," Roger Maris Jr. said.

NEW YORK (AP)—All Roger Maris ever wanted was to be known as a good ballplayer. What he got was an asterisk.

On April 26, 1961, Maris started his journey into the record book with a home run at Detroit off right-hander Paul Foytack. There would be 60 more home runs and much anguish to come.

The New York Yankees' lineup that season was filled with home run hitters: Maris, Mickey Mantle, Yogi Berra, Moose Skowron, Elston Howard and Johnny Blanchard. Maris was happiest when he was just a face in the crowd.

After finishing third in 1959, the Yankees reshaped their team and acquired the little-known Maris from Kansas City with Kent Hadley and Joe DeMaestri for Don Larsen, Hank Bauer, Marv Throneberry and Norm Siebern.

During the winter meetings of 1959, the Pittsburgh Pirates almost traded shortstop Dick Groat to Kansas City for Maris. When the deal couldn't be worked out, the Yankees made their offer.

Maris hit two home runs in his first game as a Yankee in 1960, and went on to finish with 39 homers, 112 RBIs and was named the American League MVP ahead of Mantle. There would soon be a race of another kind with Mantle.

By the end of July 1961, Maris had 40 homers and was in a chase with Mantle to catch Babe Ruth's hallowed record of 60 homers hit in 1927.

On July 17, 1961, commissioner Ford Frick ruled that Ruth's record would stand unless bettered within a 154-game limit, since that was the schedule in 1927. Maris hit 59 homers in the Yankees' first 155 games.

"I never wanted all this notoriety," Maris said during the 1961 season.

NOT EVERYONE CHEERED NO. 62
By BOB MOEN
Associated Press Writer

FARGO, N.D. (AP) -- When the local hero's home run record fell Tuesday night, Orv Kelly did not move out of his recliner.

No cheering. No clapping. Just one four-letter word.

"Well, that takes care of that," said Kelly, after Mark McGwire hit No. 62 to break Roger Maris' record.

McGwire's home run was hard to watch for Kelly, who first met Maris in 1951.

Fargo is Maris' hometown, his burial place and where his museum is located, and many here didn't want to see his record broken. Kelly was among those here who didn't want to see the record go down even though he knew it was coming.

The license plate on Kelly's Lincoln Continental reads "61 in 61" for the 61 home runs Maris hit in 1961, setting the record that would stand for 37 years.

"I was content to be known as a good ballplayer. Maybe hit 25 to 30 home runs a year, drive in 100 runs and bat somewhere between .290 and .300. And I wanted to help win pennants."

Maris did that, helping to make the Yankees AL champions from 1960-64. Twice in that span they also won the World Series. He did it by more than hitting home runs, too.

"I think a lot of people forget what a good all-around player Roger Maris was," Mantle said in 1991. "He was a great outfielder, had a good arm and was a good baserunner. He just didn't like all that attention. He was really a private kinda of guy."

Mantle and Maris, the M&M Boys, got all sorts of attention as they took aim at Ruth's record in the summer of '61. Their photos, together and solo, were all over the place and the media crush increased as Maris reached 51 homers entering September.

"I don't think the Yankees wanted me to break Ruth's record," Maris said after his retirement following the 1968 season. "They favored Mickey Mantle to break it."

Mantle hit 54 home runs in 1961 and was keeping pace with Maris until an injury sidelined him for the last two weeks of the season.

"I was used to all the attention and the press in New York by then," Mantle said. "It was tough for me when I came here at first because Casey (Stengel) was telling everybody about me and how I was going to take Joe DiMaggio's place. But Roger was from a small town and didn't handle all the attention well."

With Mantle out of the picture, all the cameras were turned on Maris in the closing days of 1961. It wasn't easy to get him to smile, either.

In game No. 155 on Sept. 20, Maris hit his 59th homer at Baltimore off Milt Pappas, falling one short of Ruth's number in 154 games.

"I didn't make the schedule and do you know any other records that have been broken since the 162-game schedule that have an asterisk? I don't," Maris said at the time. "Frick decided on the asterisk after I had about 50 homers and looked like I'd break Ruth's record."

Maris' 60th homer came in the Yankees' 159th game on September 26 off Baltimore's Jack Fisher. In the final game of the season, he hit his dramatic 61st homer in the fourth inning on a pitch from Boston's Tracy Stallard. After Maris circled the bases, the 23,154 at Yankee Stadium kept cheering and his teammates had to force him up the dugout steps to tip his cap and take a bashful bow.

The ball landed in the right-

Roger Maris, New York Yankees' slugging outfielder, follows through on his swing as he hits his record-breaking 61st home run of the season. October 1, 1961 at Yankee Stadium. (AP/Wide World Photos)

field porch—Box 163 D in Section 33—and was caught by 19-year-old Sal Durante of Brooklyn. For his historic catch, Durante won $5,000 and a round trip vacation to Sacramento, California.

What Roger Maris got out of it was much less uncertain.

"It would have been a helluva lot more fun if I had never hit those 61 home runs," Maris once said. "Some guys love the life of a celebrity. Some of them would have walked down Fifth Avenue in their Yankee uniforms if they could. But all it brought me was headaches."

As the years passed, most forgot Frick's asterisk and accepted Maris as the single-season home

run champ. After his retirement at 33 from St. Louis, Maris ran a successful beer business until his death from lymph-gland cancer in 1985.

He made very few visits back to Yankee Stadium and still found the attention of the record as difficult to handle as a flyball in the sun.

"I always come across as being bitter," Maris said shortly before his death. "I'm not bitter. People were very reluctant to give me any credit.

"I thought hitting 61 home runs was something. But everyone backed off. Why, I don't know. Maybe I wasn't the chosen one, but I was the one who got the record."

SEPTEMBER 4

CATCHING A PIECE OF IMMORTALITY

By JIM LITKE
AP Sports Writer

If he knew then what he knows now.

Sal Durante has driven a school bus for three decades. But he earned a degree in chaos before that. On October 1, 1961, he caught Roger Maris' 61st home run of the season.

Durante was 19 at the time, working in an auto-parts store in Brooklyn. He was sitting 15 rows deep in the right-field bleachers at Yankee Stadium—seat No. 4 , Box 163D, Section 33—next to the girl he would soon wed. She paid $2.50 for his ticket, as well as for hers and his cousin's and a girlfriend. It was the last game of the season, only the second time all year he'd been to the ballpark.

Maris was batting in the fourth when Boston pitcher Tracy Stallard threw one ball outside and another in the dirt, setting off a chorus of boos. Maris leaned into the next pitch and drove it 360 feet from home plate. It was a clothesline shot, right at Durante. He saw it coming all the way.

"My first thought was to give Roger the baseball," he recalled in 1998 from his Staten Island home in New York City.

Just hand it over?

"Yeah," he said. "I guess it was a different time. Money wasn't the first thing on my mind at the time."

Safety was. But it was nowhere near the concern it will be when Mark McGwire or Sammy Sosa

closes in on Maris the way the beleaguered Yankee outfielder closed in on Babe Ruth.

Kevin Hallinan, the former FBI agent who heads security for the commissioner's office, says there will be local security and police forces in addition to his own men everywhere McGwire and Sosa play for the rest of the season. His staff has been studying computer printouts of where each slugger hits his homers in every ballpark, and studied photographs of those sections in detail. That's where the biggest number of his men will be.

"In baseball terms," Hallinan said, "it's playing the percentages."

When he hears about those plans, Durante chuckles. He pulled in Maris' homer and fell into the row above his. He got smacked around a little, but by twisting from side to side, he made sure nobody could grab him. By the time he got up, two security men from the ballclub were flanking him.

The security men escorted him out of the stands, through the bullpen in right field and down the runway that leads to the Yankee dugout. Maris was waiting there, wearing an expression Durante describes nearly four decades later as "thoughtful."

"Somebody said, 'Roger, the kid wants to give you the ball.' He told me, 'Keep it. Make whatever you can on it.' I'll never forget that moment."

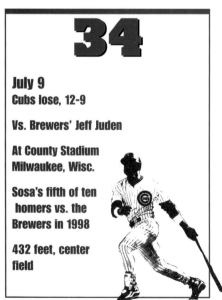

34

July 9
Cubs lose, 12-9

Vs. Brewers' Jeff Juden

At County Stadium
Milwaukee, Wisc.

Sosa's fifth of ten homers vs. the Brewers in 1998

432 feet, center field

35

July 10
Cubs lose, 6-5

Vs. Brewers' Scott Karl

At County Stadium
Milwaukee, Wisc.

Sammy's homers for the sixth consecutive time in a Cubs defeat

428 feet, left field

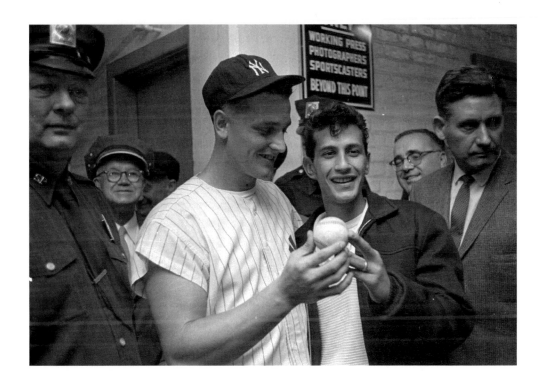

Roger Maris and Sal Durante, 19, hold Maris' 61st home run ball in the runway at New York's Yankee Stadium Oct. 1, 1961, after Durante caught the ball in the right field stands. (AP/Wide World Photos)

Today, the Shop at Home Network runs ads offering $250,000 for the record-breaking baseball. In 1961, a small item appeared in New York papers about a Sacramento, Calif., restaurant owner named Sam Gordon offering $5,000.

Even at that less-then-princely sum, a Yankee official suggested Durante leave it with the club for safekeeping. "They were afraid I'd get mugged," he said.

His story has its own happy ending.

Durante went out to California with Maris. During a photo-op, Durante gave the baseball to Gordon, who presented it to Maris and handed the teen-ager a $5,000 check. That trip and another to the West Coast were thrown into the deal. Maris later gave the ball to Cooperstown.

In today's dollars, that's $27,173.91. Back then, he used half the money to pay off his parents' debt and the rest to buy some furniture for his apartment just before he got married. Among the wedding presents he and his wife received was one from Maris.

"I think back on what he went through and I know few people knew the true Roger Maris," Durante said. "The word I come back to most often is 'thoughtful.'"

Durante had his 15 minutes of fame—and more. He showed up in the New York papers the day after. A half-dozen years ago, he recalled the event in one of the letters reprinted in Seth Swirsky's book, *Baseball Letters: A Fan's Correspondence With His Heroes*. He spent Thursday running back and forth between his home and Yankee Stadium so TV crews could film on-the-spot interviews.

Durante still is a Yankees fan, but the sad thing is he rarely has the energy or the inclination to get back to the ballpark in person.

"Today, every time you turn around, you hear money, money, money. This is what baseball turned out to be," he said.

As for his own place in the lore, Durante said he has no regrets, only second thoughts.

"I had a family. I've got grandchildren now. I'm close to retirement," he said. "I'll be honest, if it happened again, I'd like to think I wouldn't demand money. But if somebody made me an offer, I'd jump on it."

JULY 12

A KISS FOR GOOD LUCK

By R.B. FALLSTROM
AP Sports Writer

ST. LOUIS (AP)—Spending a few days with his 10-year-old son helped Mark McGwire get back to terrorizing National League pitchers.

Matthew McGwire, the St. Louis Cardinals' occasional bat boy, kissed his dad's bat for luck yesterday. Presto, McGwire ended a 21 at-bat homerless slump with a game-winning, 11th-inning upper-deck shot.

Matthew was back in southern Calforina with his mother today, but the bat still carried the magic as McGwire hit Nos. 39 and 40 in a 6-4 victory over the Houston Astros.

"He kissed my bat," McGwire said after hitting Nos. 39 and 40 in the St. Louis Cardinals' 6-4 victory over the Houston Astros. "That's what it came down to.

"But (the kiss) was still on it," McGwire said.

During the latest visit, McGwire also discovered his son likes to watch ESPN SportsCenter.

"He didn't want me to know he does it, but it's pretty cute," McGwire said. "I said 'Why do you watch it?' He said, 'To see what the Cardinals do.'"

In the first inning, McGwire hit the first pitch he saw from Sean Bergman (8-5) off the wall beyond the visitor's bullpen in left field.

He struck out in the third and drew his major league-leading 19th intentional walk in the fourth before hitting No. 40 on a 2-1 pitch from rookie Scott Elarton to lead off the seventh, a 415-foot drive.

"I've not been around too long, but the home run he hit off me was the most impressive thing I've seen in my major league career," Elarton said.

Yesterday, McGwire said he'd been only millimeters off. Today, he said it was just something he had to work through.

"There was nothing wrong with my swing," McGwire said. "You always have ups and downs. It's just part of the game. It's six months and we don't have many days off."

McGwire also broke two records for reaching 40 homers this early in the season. He bettered his own record for reaching the plateau in terms of at-bats, getting there in 281. He did it in 294 at-bats in 1996, when he finished with 52 homers.

He also reached 40 homers in the Cardinals' 90th game, bettering Babe Ruth's 1928 mark by one game.

"There's a lot of good guys I'll hopefully be passing, knock on wood," McGwire said.

"He's the same as Aaron, Ruth or Williams," Astros manager Larry Dierker said. "You've got to throw good stuff on the corners. Anything else is not acceptable."

One player McGwire said he's not like is the Baltimore Orioles' iron man.

He's scheduled to get his first day off since June 4 sometime this week.

"I'm only human, not Cal Ripken," McGwire said.

McGwire had no homers or RBIs in July and was homerless in 21 at-bats before his upper-deck shot in the 11th that won yesterday's game 4-3.

> "When he hits line drives, get the family of four out of the left field seats before they get killed."
>
> —Astros second baseman Craig Biggio on on Mark McGwire

sideNOTE

Following the July 12 game, Mark McGwire totaled 64 home runs and 133 RBIs in 135 career games with the Cardinals. He had 35 homers in his first 66 career games at Busch Stadium.

Mark McGwire acknowledges the crowd after hitting his 40th homer of the year in the seventh inning against the Houston Astros, July 12, at Busch Stadium. (AP/Wide World Photos—Leon Algee)

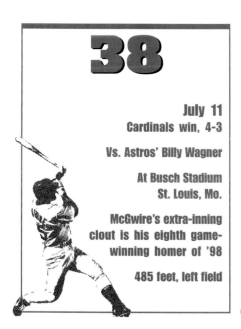

38

July 11
Cardinals win, 4-3

Vs. Astros' Billy Wagner

At Busch Stadium
St. Louis, Mo.

McGwire's extra-inning clout is his eighth game-winning homer of '98

485 feet, left field

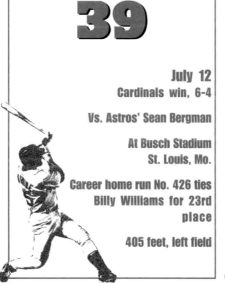

39

July 12
Cardinals win, 6-4

Vs. Astros' Sean Bergman

At Busch Stadium
St. Louis, Mo.

Career home run No. 426 ties Billy Williams for 23rd place

405 feet, left field

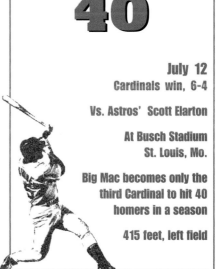

40

July 12
Cardinals win, 6-4

Vs. Astros' Scott Elarton

At Busch Stadium
St. Louis, Mo.

Big Mac becomes only the third Cardinal to hit 40 homers in a season

415 feet, left field

JULY 17

BIG MAC LAUNCHES NOS. 41 & 42

"You're not going to see a more beautiful swing on a home run than that first one. It was just classic. I'd replay that over and over again for people if they want to know how Mark does it."
— St. Louis manager Tony La Russa on Mark McGwire's 511-foot home run

ST. LOUIS (AP)—Mark McGwire got two pitches to swing at and turned them into souvenirs.

McGwire hit two homers—his 41st and 42nd—to set a major league record for most home runs by the end of July as the Cardinals beat the Los Angeles Dodgers 4-1.

"I kept telling myself tonight to be aggressive, and if I saw a pitch I could take a whack at to take a whack at it," McGwire said. "I swung the bat twice tonight. I saw two strikes and hit two home runs."

McGwire could not have been any more aggressive. He hit a 511-foot solo homer into the upper deck off Brian Bohanon (2-6) with two out in the first on the first pitch he saw, his first homer in five games. McGwire hit another solo shot in the eighth off Antonio Osuna to break the July mark held by Babe Ruth and Jimmie Foxx.

The homer off Bohanon was the fourth-longest since they started measuring them at Busch Stadium in 1988. McGwire also hit the other three, including the record 545-foot shot against Florida on May 16.

"I don't diagnose things like that," McGwire said. "You see it and you swing. I'm not a player that sits around and diagnoses a swing."

It was the fifth multihomer game this year and 48th of his career for McGwire, who moved within one homer of the Cardinals' team record set by Johnny Mize in 1940.

McGwire walked in his other two plate appearances, giving him a major league-leading 99 for the season. Bohanon admitted he wasn't going to give McGwire any more whacks.

"He got me in the first at-bat and in the second-at bat, I decided I wasn't going to let him hit," Bohanon said. "I decided to take my chances with (Brian) Jordan. I hate doing that, but I felt like it was the best situation."

After McGwire's home run, Bohanon only allowed a soft single to center by Gary Gaetti in the second. He lasted 5 2-3 innings, striking out six and walking two. Bohanon has dropped his first two decisions since being acquired from the Mets on July 10.

McGwire, who has four homers in nine career at-bats against Bohanon, has 66 homers in 140 career games with the Cardinals.

"He's one of the batters that I struggle against," Bohanon said. "He hits my fastball, he hits my change-up, he hits my curve ball. He's just such a dangerous threat any time he comes up. With the power he has, Yellowstone ain't going to hold him."

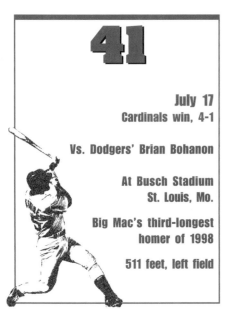

41

July 17
Cardinals win, 4-1

Vs. Dodgers' Brian Bohanon

At Busch Stadium
St. Louis, Mo.

Big Mac's third-longest homer of 1998

511 feet, left field

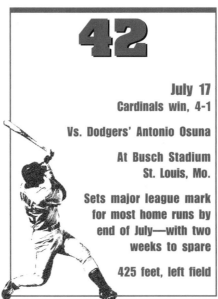

42

July 17
Cardinals win, 4-1

Vs. Dodgers' Antonio Osuna

At Busch Stadium
St. Louis, Mo.

Sets major league mark for most home runs by end of July—with two weeks to spare

425 feet, left field

Mark McGwire connects for his 41st homer of the year—a 511-footer—in the first inning against the Los Angeles Dodgers. (AP/Wide World Photos—Mary Butkus)

36

July 17
Cubs win, 6-1

Vs. Marlins' Kirt Ojala

At Pro Player
Stadium
Miami, Fla.

Sosa's first homer
in a Cubs victory
since June 20th

440 feet, center
field

43

July 20
Cardinals win, 13-1

Vs. Padres' Brian Boehringer

At Qualcomm Stadium
San Diego, Calif.

McGwire ties Johnny Mize's
Cardinals single-season
home-run record, set
in 1930

458 feet, left field

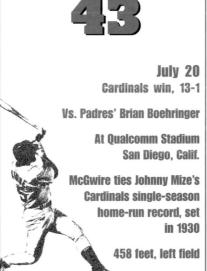

37

July 22
Cubs win, 9-5

Vs. Expos' Miguel Batista

At Wrigley Field
Chicago, Ill.

His 37th homer in
'98 is one more
than he hit in all of
'97

365 feet, right field

JULY 26

McGWIRE ENDS SLUMP WITH 44TH HOMER

By AARON J. LOPEZ
AP Sports Writer

> "I'm just learning the history of the Cardinals. I was stuck on the West Coast for 11 years and didn't really know much about their history, but now I do and I'm happy to be part of it."
>
> — Mark McGwire after hitting home run No. 44

DENVER (AP)—Feeling the effects of playing in 18 straight games since the All-Star break, Mark McGwire was itching for a day off. He made history instead.

McGwire ended an 0-for-16 slump with his major league-leading 44th homer as the St. Louis Cardinals beat Colorado 3-1 to snap the Rockies' five-game winning streak.

"I'm not Cal Ripken. I'm not going to play every day," McGwire said. "It's for me and for the better. I'm looking for myself to finish the year strong. I'm not going to burn myself out for anybody else."

"I've been doing it the last couple years and playing a lot of games. Everybody talks about me staying healthy. This is a good way to stay healthy."

"I would have loved to have had the day off today," said McGwire, who homered for the first time in six games. "But look what happened. I ran into one."

The homer, a 452-foot shot in the fourth inning, broke the Cardinals' mark of 43 set by Johnny Mize in 1940 and was McGwire's first since last Monday as he added to his major league record for home runs before August 1.

It was McGwire's only hit of the game—he went 1-for-4—and his first hit of any kind since last Monday. His 0-for-16 drought was his longest of the season.

"I'm not pressing at all," McGwire said. "I'm tired, period. Everybody goes through it. Just because you're not getting hits doesn't mean you're having bad at-bats. There's too much emphasis on numbers."

McGwire did not get to keep home run ball No. 44. The man who caught it said he wanted to keep it because he had a dream it would happen. That's good enough for me," said McGwire, who autographed the ball. "I'm into that stuff. I hope he has more dreams."

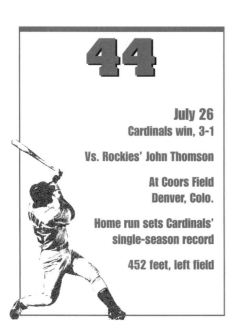

44

July 26
Cardinals win, 3-1

Vs. Rockies' John Thomson

At Coors Field
Denver, Colo.

Home run sets Cardinals'
single-season record

452 feet, left field

38

July 26
Cubs win, 3-1

Vs. Mets' Rick Reed

At Wrigley Field
Chicago, Ill.

Sosa and McGwire hit homers on the same day for the 12th time in '98

420 feet, center field

Mark McGwire watches the flight of his 44th home run as it sails out of Denver's Coors Field. (AP/Wide World Photos—David Zalubowski)

John Thomson (5-7), activated from the disabled list before the game, retired the first 11 hitters he faced before McGwire hit the first pitch onto the left-field concourse.

"The home run he hit was a slider," Thomson said. "It wasn't something like a strikeout pitch or anything. I just wanted to throw him a strike and get ahead of him. He's hit a lot of home runs. That's just his game."

It was McGwire's fifth homer in 10 career games at Coors Field. He is on pace to hit 69 homers, which would shatter Roger Maris' record of 61 in 1961.

JULY 27

SOSA HEATS UP IN PHOENIX

By BOB BAUM
AP Sports Writer

PHOENIX (AP)—Look out, Sammy Sosa is heating up again.

After his record 20 home runs in June, Sosa had a mere four in July until he homered against the Mets in Chicago yesterday. Tonight, he hit two more—including his first career grand slam—as the Cubs beat the Arizona Diamondbacks 6-2.

That gives him 40 home runs and 102 RBIs.

"I've been swinging too hard, trying to hit the home run," he said.

"I said to myself I have to be more relaxed and go out there and make good contact. I'm happy about it. I just want to keep it going."

His two homers drove in all of Chicago's runs as the Cubs won for the eighth time in 10 games. Sosa's 40 homers puts him just four behind Mark McGwire and he has four more RBIs than the St. Louis slugger. But Sosa said Roger Maris' home run record of 61 is McGwire's to break, not his.

"I've said it all along, McGwire is the man," Sosa said.

Sosa's eighth-inning shot to straightaway center field ended the longest streak of homers without a slam from the start of a career in major league history.

"Thank God," he said, "I'm not going to have to hear that no more."

Sosa had hit 246 homers without a grand slam before he hit reliever Alan Embree's first pitch 438 feet to center. Earlier, his two-run opposite field homer tied it at 2 in the sixth.

"That's twice he's pulled my pants down and embarrassed me," said Embree, who also gave up Sosa's 20th June home run. "I have to figure out a way to get that guy out."

Chicago manager Jim Riggleman said Sosa was razzed a little bit by his teammates for finally hitting a grand slam.

"I'm sure he's glad to get that monkey off his back because it was really just a fluke thing that he hadn't hit one," Riggleman said.

Sosa matched his career best of 40 homers and eclipsed the 100 RBI mark for the fourth consecutive season, all with two months to go.

"The difference this year is I'm in a different situation," Sosa said. "When you play on a winning team, everything is easy. You want to go out to the ballpark early and you want to win the game."

39

July 27
Cubs win, 6-2

Vs. Diamondbacks' Willie Blair

At Bank One Ballpark Phoenix, Ariz.

Sosa's first of two gives him 29 multi-homer games in his career

347 feet, right field

40

July 27
Cubs win, 6-2

Vs. Diamondbacks' Alan Embree

At Bank One Ballpark Phoenix, Ariz.

Sammy's first grand slam home run of his career

438 feet, center field

Sammy Sosa gestures as he begins his home-run trot after he slugged a grand slam homer against the Arizona Diamondbacks. (AP/Wide World Photos—Ken Levine)

AUGUST 12

THE BABE

By HAL BOCK
AP Sports Writer

The crowd arrived early, a throng so large it spilled out of Yankee Stadium and onto the adjacent streets. The people lined up side-by-side, four and five abreast, winding around the ballpark just as they had so many times before for big games.

This time was different, though. There was no buzz of anticipation, none of the customary pregame excitement so familiar at the Stadium. There was only silence and the soft shuffling of feet as the people moved slowly into the building to pay their last respects.

Babe Ruth was dead.

Fifty years ago Sunday, Ruth's fight for life ended in Manhattan's Memorial Hospital, now known as Sloan Kettering. His body was ravaged by cancer, his once huge frame left gaunt by the disease. He was 53.

For two days, mourners filed by his coffin in a steady stream that began early in the morning and stretched until midnight. When it ended, 77,000 people had come to say farewell to an American hero, a baseball player lying in state like a president, in the ballpark he defined.

For two years, Ruth had been in and out of hospitals, battling the disease, progressively deteriorating.

His trouble started with a persistent pain over his left eye, dismissed at first as a sinus headache. But this headache wouldn't go away. The nagging pain caused Ruth to be admitted to New York's French Hospital in November 1946. Doctors decided the problem was a nerve in his neck.

On January 6, 1947, the Babe underwent surgery. Surgeons found a malignant tumor on the left side of his neck. They removed as much of the growth as they could but the cancer had spread and it was just a matter of time.

Ruth lost 80 pounds after the surgery and said there were times he thought he would die right there in the hospital. He was in constant pain and only doses of morphine provided any relief for the man who once had been the centerpiece of baseball.

Shocked by Ruth's condition, baseball decided to honor him on April 27 that year. Every major league ballpark held a salute to the ailing slugger.

Ruth, weak and frail, was driven to Yankee Stadium for the ceremonies and helped onto the field.

He wore a cap over his thinning, white hair and a camel's hair coat that hung loosely on his once powerful body. As the ceremonies began, he slowly moved over to umpires Bill Summers and Bill McGowan, the only ones still active from his era.

A week later, Summers recalled the moment.

"He whispers to me, 'There's only a few of us left, right, kid?'" he said.

Summers said he nodded and looked away.

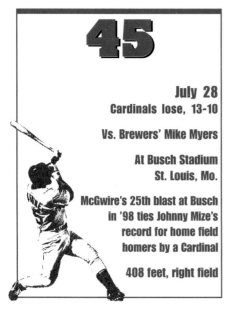

45

July 28

Cardinals lose, 13-10

Vs. Brewers' Mike Myers

**At Busch Stadium
St. Louis, Mo.**

McGwire's 25th blast at Busch in '98 ties Johnny Mize's record for home field homers by a Cardinal

408 feet, right field

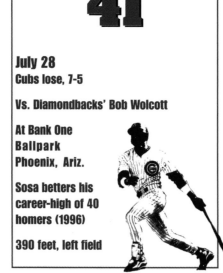

41

July 28

Cubs lose, 7-5

Vs. Diamondbacks' Bob Wolcott

At Bank One Ballpark Phoenix, Ariz.

Sosa betters his career-high of 40 homers (1996)

390 feet, left field

Ruth's voice was all but gone, but he spoke to the crowd in a hoarse whisper. "You know how bad my voice sounds," he said. "Well, it feels just as bad. There's been so many lovely things said about me. I'm glad I had the opportunity to thank everybody. Thank you."

This was 20 years after Ruth had been the toast of baseball, a hulking slugger on pipestem thin legs who set a record with 60 home runs in a season.

He was perhaps the most compelling and captivating character in the Golden Age of Sports, the age of Dempsey and Grange, Tilden and Rockne.

He hit a record 714 home runs and had a lifetime batting average of .341. "I could have hit .600," he once said, "but I would have had to hit singles. The people were paying for me to hit home runs."

So he hit home runs. And with them came a flip side— 1,330 strikeouts.

Ruth once said, "I swing big, with everything I've got. I hit big or I miss big. I like to live as big as I can."

And now he was dying.

By June 1948, it was obvious that he did not have much time left. The Yankees celebrated the Stadium's silver anniversary June 13 and retired Ruth's No. 3 that day.

Old teammates gathered again, just as they had a year earlier.

This time, the farewells would be permanent. Ruth was helped into his old uniform and came on the field, a broken man, hunched over, leaning on a bat for support. It was a poignant moment as the Babe, his voice husky, spoke with tears

Babe Ruth, wearing his famed No. 3 uniform for the last time, bows to acknowledge the cheers at Yankee Stadium. The Bambino's number was retired during the June 13, 1948, observance of the 25th anniversary of the opening of the stadium. (AP/Wide World Photo)

streaming down his face.

"Ladies and gentlemen," he rasped, "I just want to say one thing.

"I am proud I hit the first home run here against Boston in 1923. It is marvelous to see these 13 or 14 players who were my teammates going back 25 years. I'm telling you, it makes me proud and happy to be here. Thank you."

Ruth was helped from the field to the dressing room. As he rested there, old pal and teammate Joe Dugan joined him. Dugan asked how Ruth was doing.

"Joe, I'm gone," he replied. "I'm gone, Joe."

Both men cried.

Eleven days later, on June 24,

Ruth was admitted to Memorial Hospital, presumably for observation and rest.

Time was running out.

On July 21, he received the last rites of the Roman Catholic Church. On August 11, he was placed on the critical list. On August 15, Ford Frick, a longtime friend and then president of the National League, came to see him.

In his seminal biography of Ruth, Robert Creamer gives Frick's account of the visit.

"It was a terrible moment. Ruth was so thin, it was unbelievable.

"He had been such a big man, and his arms were just skinny little bones and his face was so haggard."

The next day, Babe Ruth died.

After laying in state at Yankee Stadium for two days, Ruth's body was moved to St. Patrick's Cathedral for the funeral on August 20.

On a rainy, hot summer's day, the streets around the chapel were choked with 75,000 people. Inside the church, pallbearers prepared to carry the mahogany coffin to the hearse for the 30-mile trip through Manhattan, into The Bronx, past Yankee Stadium one last time, to Gate of Heaven Cemetery in Hawthorne, N.Y.

Two of the mourners were old Ruth teammates, Dugan and Waite Hoyt.

As he lifted the casket, Dugan, suffering in the heat, whispered to Hoyt, "I'd give a hundred bucks for an ice cold beer."

Hoyt smiled and glanced at the coffin.

"So would the Babe," he said.

JULY 31

McGWIRE'S FIRST YEAR A PRODUCTIVE ONE

By ED SHEARER
AP Sports Writer

"No way. How could a child sit back and say I'm going to break Roger Maris' record?"
—Mark McGwire, after being asked if he thought as a youngster he'd be challenging the home run mark

42

July 31
Cubs win, 9-1

Vs. Rockies' Jamey Wright

**At Wrigley Field
Chicago, Ill.**

Sammy's 29th homer of June and July

375 feet, right field

ATLANTA (AP)—Completing his first year with the St. Louis Cardinals, Mark McGwire put up statistics that were nothing less than staggering.

McGwire, acquired from Oakland last July 31, has 69 homers, 142 RBIs and a .280 average in 153 games for St. Louis.

He has 45 homers, 16 behind Roger Maris' record, and is on pace to hit 67.

In Atlanta, he finds himself hitting against a pitching staff that leads the majors with a 3.35 ERA.

"I always look forward to facing the best in the game," McGwire said before going 0-for-3 and striking out twice against four-time Cy Young Award winner Greg Maddux. "If not the best, he's one of the best in the game. He throws nothing but strikes and nothing straight."

McGwire again insisted that he's not thinking about the record

Through his 45th homer, the average distance of Mark McGwire's blasts was 424.4 feet. Of the 16 home runs he hit from No. 30 through No. 45, Big Mac walloped 15 of them 405 feet or more, averaging 437.4 feet per homer during that 16-homer span.

now, adding that if he got to 50 by September, "you can sit down and think about it."

During a pregame news conference, McGwire was asked about the first home run he ever hit in his life.

"I think it felt pretty good," he said. "I was 10. It was my first at-bat in Little League. I swung and closed my eyes, and it went out."

He said he certainly didn't start thinking about Maris' record then.

Fans, as they have all season, arrived early to watch McGwire take batting practice.

"I've been dealing with this ever since I broke in in '87," McGwire said. "I've done this for 11 years in the American League. Now it's a show in the National League. What counts is what happens in the game."

Mark McGwire does his trademark behind-the-back stretch.
(AP/Wide World Photos—John Gaps III)

CATCHING "THE" BALL

By ARNIE STAPLETON
AP Sports Writer

"If somebody's going to hold this ball hostage for a dollar sign, you can take it home with you. There is not a piece of memorabilia that's worth a dime."

—Mark McGwire, after being asked if he'd pay for home run ball No. 62

MILWAUKEE (AP)—If Mark McGwire breaks Roger Maris' record, somebody else will have to pony up the big bucks for home run ball No. 62.

"I wouldn't pay a dime for it," he said.

Joseph Burr, a sports memorabilia collector from suburban Milwaukee, likens the record-breaking ball to a winning lottery ticket.

"Some kid's going to become an instant millionaire," he said. "It's easily over $1 million."

McGwire, stuck on 45 homers for nearly a week entering Wednesday night's game at Milwaukee, can't fathom that.

"Let me ask you, who's going to pay the money?" he said. "I'm not."

But you can bet somebody else will.

After all, the founder of the Psychic Friends Network paid a cool $500,000 for Eddie Murray's 500th home run.

The St. Louis Cardinals slugger is put off by the naked greed.

"If somebody's going to put a price on a ball like that, to me that's worthless," McGwire said. "If somebody wants a bat or a jersey or a ball (in exchange), then that means something."

Unlike many other stars, McGwire refuses to enter autograph deals. With the exception of some promotions to benefit his charity, Mark McGwire Foundation for Children, McGwire doesn't sell autographs.

That's not to say he doesn't sign until his hand aches.

As he closes in on Maris' record of 61 homers, McGwire said he can't go anywhere without getting mobbed. But he won't become a recluse.

"I don't change who I am," he said. "I go out and I do what I need to do. But, you know, it's been sort of uncomfortable this year. It just seems everywhere I go somebody's tapping me on the shoulder or sliding a piece of paper on the table. Or even coming down and just sitting at your table with you."

Uninvited guests? That's what it's come to?

"Oh, yeah, quite a few times. I just ask them, 'Do you do this often?'" McGwire said with a smile.

McGwire said somebody should write a book on autograph etiquette, and he even has the title for Chapter 1.

"Just ask for the autograph," said McGwire, who doesn't like the approach, "I'm sorry to bother you, but ..." He figures if somebody really was sorry to bother him, they shouldn't be bothering him in the first place.

"I always tell people, 'You don't need to say that.' Just say, 'May I please have your autograph?'"

And most of the time, he says, you'll get it.

"Listen, you can't make everybody happy. And they have to respect my privacy. I respect theirs," McGwire said. "So, if I don't sign an

A slow-shutter exposure captures the camera flashes from all around Busch Stadium as fans attempt to record Mark McGwire's historical season. McGwire grounded out on the play. (AP/ Wide World Photos—Ed Reinke)

autograph, obviously there's a good reason why I don't sign. But I would say the majority of the time, I do it."

As for disappointments, McGwire realizes he's going to have to take a day off soon, dismaying thousands of fans.

Entering Wednesday, he hadn't homered in 24 at-bats and had struck out 10 times in his last 17 at-bats, a clear sign he's getting tired.

The remedy would be a day off, something he has done six times this season.

"Everybody says, there's a chance for him to do it if he stays healthy," McGwire said. "Well, the times that people usually get injured is when they're tired. I've always said days off go a long way. I'm not Cal Ripken."

Who, by the way, homered on the night he broke Lou Gehrig's record for consecutive games and got the ball back from the fan who caught it.

The ransom? Ripken's signature on a bat, that's all.

McGwire could live with that.

43

August 5
Cubs lose, 7-10

Vs. Diamondbacks' Andy Benes

At Wrigley Field
Chicago, Ill.

Career home run
No. 250 for
Slammin' Sammy

374 feet, left field

AUGUST 8

LANKFORD OUTSHINES THE STARS

By JIM SALTER
AP Writer

> "It's one of the greatest games I've ever been associated with. They thought they had it and we came back. We thought we had it and they came back."
> — Cubs manager Jim Riggleman

ST. LOUIS (AP)—Ray Lankford turned a miserable performance into a memorable one, following five strikeouts with two big hits in the St. Louis Cardinals' 9-8, 13-inning, win over the Chicago Cubs.

Lankford's heroics—a two-out, game-tying homer in the 11th and a game-winning single in the 13th—overshadowed homers by both men chasing Roger Maris' record. Mark McGwire hit his major league-leading 46th homer leading off the fourth. And Sammy Sosa tied the game in the ninth with a two-run shot, his 44th.

"I've never seen anything like it," St. Louis manager Tony La Russa said.

McGwire went 1-for-3 with four walks, giving him 119 on the season. Two of the walks were intentional, giving him 26. Sosa was 2-for-5 with a walk.

McGwire's homer ended a 29 at-bat drought, his longest of the season.

McGwire hit a 2-1 pitch from Cubs starter Mark Clark. The ball cleared the left field wall, about 10 feet inside the foul line. The distance was estimated at 374 feet. He needs 15 homers to tie Maris' record 61 set in 1961.

The Cardinals have 47 games remaining. Chicago has 45 games left.

"Why is everybody so worried about this?," McGwire asked. "There are more important things to worry about than Mark McGwire hitting home runs. Let's talk about the game."

It was worth talking about.

After Sosa's ninth-inning blast tied it 5-5, the Cubs seemed on their way to breaking a modest two-game losing streak when Tyler Houston hit a two-run homer in the 11th off reliever Curtis King.

But Chicago shortstop Jeff Blauser let Brian Jordan's one-out grounder go under his glove in the bottom of the inning. McGwire struck out, bringing up Lankford.

At that point, Lankford's hadn't put the ball in play—he was 0-for-5 with five strikeouts, tying a team record set by Dick Allen in 1970.

"He told me he was swinging like he had a hole in his bat," La Russa said.

But Lankford hit an opposite-field shot off Rod Beck to left to tie the game.

Again, the Cubs took the lead in the 12th on a single by Sosa, his league-leading 114th RBI of the season.

Again, the Cardinals answered. This time, catcher Eli Marrero homered off Beck.

In the 13th, reliever Dave Stevens (1-1), the Cubs' seventh pitcher, walked Pat Kelly, who stole second and went to third on Brian Jordan's single.

McGwire was walked intentionally, and the Cubs brought center-fielder Lance Johnson in as a fifth infielder. But Lankford slapped a single well to Johnson's right.

Bobby Witt (2-3), the eighth Cardinals pitcher, pitched one inning for the win.

Mark McGwire follows through on his fourth-inning solo home run against the Chicago Cubs, August 8. (AP/Wide World Photos—Leon Algee)

46

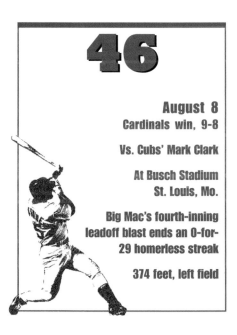

August 8
Cardinals win, 9-8

Vs. Cubs' Mark Clark

At Busch Stadium
St. Louis, Mo.

Big Mac's fourth-inning leadoff blast ends an 0-for-29 homerless streak

374 feet, left field

44

August 8
Cubs lose, 9-8

Vs. Cardinals' Rich Croushere

At Busch Stadium
St. Louis, Mo.

Sammy's 26th home run of 400 feet or more

400 feet, left field

August 8th's attendance of 48,064 was the largest crowd of the season at Busch Stadium and put the Cardinals over the 2 million mark through 53 home dates. The team is on track to draw more than 3 million fans for the third time in its history. A clause in Mark McGwire's contract pays him $1 per ticket for each ticket sold above 2.8 million.

AUGUST 10

SAMMY TIES BIG MAC FOR THE HOME RUN LEAD

By ROB GLOSTER
AP Sports Writer

> "Knowing how hard it is to hit a baseball and seeing what he's doing, it's an amazing thing."
>
> **—Cubs manager Jim Riggleman**

SAN FRANCISCO (AP)—After chasing him all season, Sammy Sosa finally caught Mark McGwire—at least for a night. Next up, Roger Maris.

Sosa hit his 45th and 46th homers to tie McGwire for the major league lead as the Chicago Cubs beat the San Francisco Giants 8-5.

But Sosa, who has hit 37 homers in 66 games since May 25, said McGwire's still the one to watch in the chase for Maris' record of 61 homers in a season.

"I still believe McGwire's the man, no matter what happens," Sosa said. "He's the man. I still believe he's going to come back and keep rolling. I know he can do it."

Sosa's first homer of the night, a towering blast into the first row of the left-field bleachers in the fifth inning, was the first of three consecutive solo shots by the Cubs.

His second one, a solo blast over the center-field bleachers estimated at 480 feet in the seventh, pulled him even for the first time this season with McGwire—who went homerless in St. Louis' loss to the New York Mets tonight.

Though the wind was blowing out at 20 mph during the early part of the game, players said it started blowing toward right in the middle innings and was blowing toward the plate late in the game.

After the game, Cubs center fielder Brant Brown was still marveling at Sosa's second shot.

"He crushed that ball," Brown said. "That one and the one down the line at Wrigley that hit the house, those are the two farthest balls I've seen him hit all year."

"That ball to center field was absolutely on afterburners," San Francisco's Jeff Kent said. "I was glad we went after him, but he ended up kicking our butts tonight."

Cubs manager Jim Riggleman called Sosa's second homer "majestic."

Sosa's first homer began a streak of three straight homers in a span of eight pitches. Mark Grace followed with his 13th homer and Henry Rodriguez added his 28th.

It was the sixth time in Cubs history the club had three consecutive homers.

Sosa went 2-for-5 while increasing his NL-leading RBI total to 116. He struck out in the first and third innings, and popped to second in the ninth.

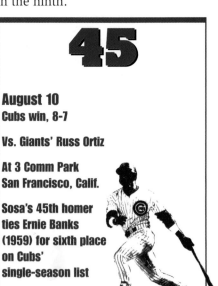

45

August 10
Cubs win, 8-7

Vs. Giants' Russ Ortiz

At 3 Comm Park
San Francisco, Calif.

Sosa's 45th homer ties Ernie Banks (1959) for sixth place on Cubs' single-season list

361 feet, left field

Sammy Sosa watches the ball leave the park as he hits his 45th home run at 3 Comm Park in San Francisco. (AP/Wide World Photos—Thearon Henderson)

46

August 10
Cubs win, 8-7

Vs. Giants' Chris Brock

At 3 Comm Park
San Francisco, Calif.

Sosa's 30th multi-homer game of his career

480 feet, center field

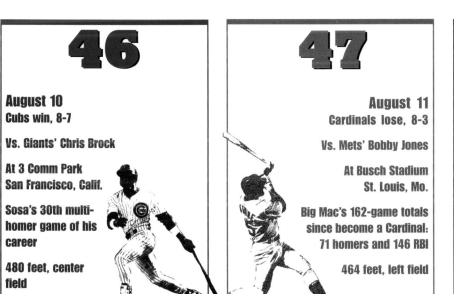

47

August 11
Cardinals lose, 8-3

Vs. Mets' Bobby Jones

At Busch Stadium
St. Louis, Mo.

Big Mac's 162-game totals since become a Cardinal: 71 homers and 146 RBI

464 feet, left field

47

August 16
Cubs win, 2-1

Vs. Astros' Sean Bergman

At The Astrodome
Houston, Tex.

Sammy's 47th blast ties Ernie Banks (1958) for fifth place on Cubs' season list

360 feet, right field

AUGUST 19

McGWIRE PULLS AHEAD

By NANCY ARMOUR
AP Sports Writer

"THAT's why he is the man."

—Sammy Sosa on Mark McGwire after his two home run game

CHICAGO (AP)—First Sosa. Then McGwire. Then McGwire again. A head-to-head matchup between baseball's home run leaders doesn't get much better than this.

Mark McGwire answered Sammy Sosa's home run with two of his own, hitting Nos. 48 and 49 in consecutive at-bats to give the Cardinals an 8-6 victory over the Cubs in 10 innings. Sosa hit his 48th homer in the fifth inning.

McGwire had been homerless in 20 at-bats, hitting his last one August 11.

"I'm just happy I can help the Cardinals. I've been an ornament the last month," McGwire said. "I'm just happy to contribute, especially in this big series."

After tying the game at 6 in the eighth, McGwire homered to center field in the 10th. Ray Lankford, batting after McGwire, hit a solo home run to make it 8-6.

"THAT's why he is the man," Sosa said, repeating what he's been saying all season.

The Cubs blew a chance to win it in the bottom of the inning.

With two outs, Mark Grace singled, then moved to third on Henry Rodriguez's double. Juan Acevedo intentionally walked Jose Hernandez to load the bases, but Manny Alexander popped up to McGwire to end the game.

"It's exciting for the fans, but we're kind of agonizing," Cubs manager Jim Riggleman said. "We let things slip away."

This was exactly the kind of game fans hoped to see when McGwire and Sosa took the field together. The two were hitless in their first matchup Tuesday night, going a combined 0-for-9, and it looked like another disappointing day early on. Though he hit a long ball to the left field warning track in his first at-bat, McGwire was 0-for-2 with two walks. Sosa struck out and singled.

"It's a tough thing to do when everybody wants it to be done," McGwire said. "When you get a pitch to hit, it doesn't necessarily mean you are going to hit it."

The hitting show began in the fifth inning. Sosa took Kent Bottenfield's first pitch and sent it over the left-field wall for No. 48, a two-run homer that put the Cubs ahead 6-2. Sosa now has a major league-leading 121 RBIs for the season, a career high. He had 119 RBIs in 1997 and 1995.

McGwire watched from first as Sosa broke into his home run trot and the Wrigley Field crowd of 39,689 went wild. The crowd chanted "Sam-my, Sam-my," and gave Sosa a standing ovation as he rounded the bases. Fans bowed as Sosa walked down the steps of the Cubs dugout, and he came out a few seconds later to wave at the still-cheering fans.

McGwire paid homage to Sosa, too. When Sosa reached first base after being walked in the seventh inning, a smiling McGwire tapped his chest and kissed his fingers, imitating Sosa's salute to his mother and the late Harry Caray.

"Even though I'm on the other side and we're playing against him and I want to see our team win, it's just awesome to see that kind of talent and the way he goes about his business," McGwire said. "He's quite a player."

McGwire, who's led the majors in homers almost all year, wasn't about to be outdone, however. With one out and the Cardinals trailing 6-5 in the eighth, McGwire slammed a 3-1 pitch out of the ballpark and onto Waveland Avenue. Fans in left field turned around to watch the ball bounce as a grinning McGwire trotted around the bases.

He bumped fists with his teammates as he returned to the dugout, and Cardinal fans bowed.

And McGwire wasn't done. With the score still tied in the 10th, he sent a 2-0 pitch into the shrubbery in the center field stands. He finished the day 2-for-4 with two walks. Sosa was 2-for-4 with a walk.

Though McGwire is only one home run away from 50—his benchmark for someone to make a legitimate run at Roger Maris' single-season record of 61—he's still downplaying talk of the record. All this back-and-forth competition is fun, but wait until the season is over.

"There is a long way to go. There are six weeks," he said. "Until that last out of the last game of the season, that's when it means something. There is a long way to go."

But this game meant something, too. Even McGwire and Sosa, whose homer was his 48th, admit they enjoy watching each other hit home runs as much as the next baseball fan. This gave them a front-row seat for the action.

Mark McGwire blows a trademark Sammy Sosa kiss to the Chicago slugger as the two meet at Wrigley Field. (AP/Wide World Photos—John Gaps III)

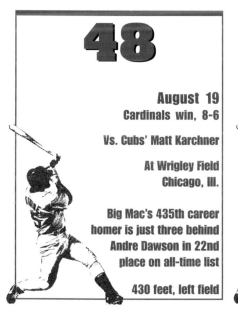

48

August 19
Cardinals win, 8-6

Vs. Cubs' Matt Karchner

At Wrigley Field
Chicago, Ill.

Big Mac's 435th career homer is just three behind Andre Dawson in 22nd place on all-time list

430 feet, left field

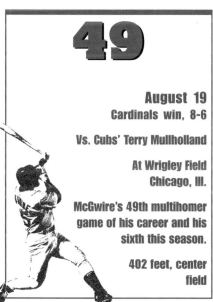

49

August 19
Cardinals win, 8-6

Vs. Cubs' Terry Mullholland

At Wrigley Field
Chicago, Ill.

McGwire's 49th multihomer game of his career and his sixth this season.

402 feet, center field

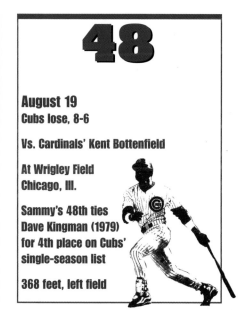

48

August 19
Cubs lose, 8-6

Vs. Cardinals' Kent Bottenfield

At Wrigley Field
Chicago, Ill.

Sammy's 48th ties Dave Kingman (1979) for 4th place on Cubs' single-season list

368 feet, left field

BIG MAC MAKES HISTORY IN BIG APPLE

By TOM WITHERS
AP Sports Writer

"People always have been fascinated with home run hitters, with pitchers who throw the ball 100 mph and golfers who can hit the ball 300 yards."

—Mark McGwire

NEW YORK (AP)—Mark McGwire couldn't have picked a better place to make history.

In the city where Roger Maris and Babe Ruth became forever linked by hitting home runs, McGwire broke one of Ruth's records and moved a little closer to Maris' on Thursday night.

Just across town from Yankee Stadium, where Maris hit his record 61st homer to break Ruth's mark 37 years ago, McGwire hit Nos. 50 and 51 as the St. Louis Cardinals split a doubleheader with the New York Mets.

McGwire became the first player in history to hit 50 home runs in three consecutive seasons with a high drive in the seventh inning of the first game, a 2-0 Cardinals win.

"Anytime you deal with history, what can you say?" McGwire said.

"I never dreamt this when I as a kid, I never dreamt this when I was a minor leaguer, college player. I thought about it going into the season, and I reached it."

McGwire, who has hit four homers in his last three games, has said since spring training that the only way he or anyone else could have a legitimate shot at catching Maris would be if they had 50 homers by September 1.

It's August 21, Mark. What do you think now?

"I'd have to say that I do have a shot," he said. "But I know it's going to be tough."

Let the countdown begin at 11 with 36 games remaining. If McGwire believes he's got a chance, then so should everyone else. After all, he hit 15 homers last September for St. Louis.

After a minor lapse—he hit his 48th and 49th homers on Wednesday to snap a 28 at-bat homerless streak—McGwire is right back on Maris' pace.

"I'm getting my second wind," he said. "I've been feeling pretty decent at the plate, and it's just a matter of getting the pitches to hit."

McGwire wasted no time hitting No. 51, connecting in the first inning of the second game, but St. Louis blew a three-run lead and lost 5-4.

After Brian Jordan led off the seventh inning of the first game with a homer, McGwire made history by sending a 2-1 pitch over the wall in left-center. McGwire pumped his right fist above his head as he rounded first base as the Shea Stadium crowd of 40,308 saluted him with a rousing standing ovation.

"I have to thank the fans here in New York," he said. "It was tremendous, I mean, wow, what a reception. They were rooting me on."

sideNOTE

Mark McGwire said he'd like to go back in time to see how difficult it was for Ruth in 1927 and Maris in 1961 to break the singularly most important individual record in sports.

"I wish I could go back and play with him (Ruth)," said McGwire. "Today's baseball is so much different because of the specialty pitching. Back then, the starting pitcher usually went nine innings and you sometimes saw the same pitcher twice in a series."

Mark McGwire is greeted at the dugout after he hit his 51st home run of the season in the first inning of the second game of a doubleheader against the Mets, August 20, at Shea Stadium in New York. (AP/Wide World Photos—Osamu Honda)

50

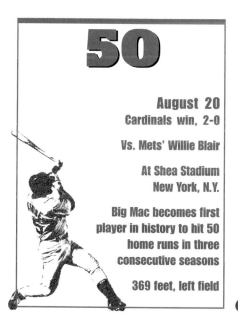

August 20
Cardinals win, 2-0

Vs. Mets' Willie Blair

At Shea Stadium
New York, N.Y.

Big Mac becomes first player in history to hit 50 home runs in three consecutive seasons

369 feet, left field

51

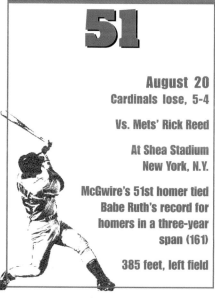

August 20
Cardinals lose, 5-4

Vs. Mets' Rick Reed

At Shea Stadium
New York, N.Y.

McGwire's 51st homer tied Babe Ruth's record for homers in a three-year span (161)

385 feet, left field

49

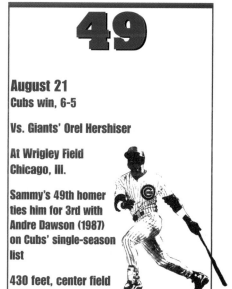

August 21
Cubs win, 6-5

Vs. Giants' Orel Hershiser

At Wrigley Field
Chicago, Ill.

Sammy's 49th homer ties him for 3rd with Andre Dawson (1987) on Cubs' single-season list

430 feet, center field

AUGUST 22

PIRATES FANS BECOME McGWIRE FANS

By ALAN ROBINSON
AP Sports Writer

PITTSBURGH (AP)—As he closes in on Roger Maris' record, Mark McGwire took care of one of Babe Ruth's, too.

McGwire broke Ruth's record for homers in three consecutive seasons with his 52nd this year as the Pittsburgh Pirates beat the St. Louis Cardinals 14-4.

McGwire has 33 games to match Roger Maris' record of 61 homers, set in 1961. He powered an 0-2 pitch by Francisco Cordova into the right-center stands in the first inning, a 477-foot drive that was the longest in Three Rivers Stadium this season. It was only his third opposite-field homer all season.

McGwire has 162 homers in three seasons, including 52 in 1996 and 58 in 1997. Ruth hit 161 from 1926-28.

"What can I say? I've surpassed anything I ever expected," McGwire said. "Obviously, it means a lot, but I can't let myself think about it because I've got to come back tomorrow."

McGwire set a Cardinals' record for homers in consecutive seasons (76) and an NL record for most homers by a first baseman in one season. Johnny Mize hit 51 in 1947.

McGwire's 52 homers are the most before September.

"I'm glad he delivered. I take my hat off to Cordova," Cardinals manager Tony La Russa said. "He challenged him. It was him against Mac and that's how it's supposed to be. It's what people pay to see: Competition, and that definitely was."

Before homering, McGwire was only 6-for-28 with only one homer against the Pirates. They seemed so intent on pitching around him during a homerless three-game series in St. Louis last weekend that Pirates manager Gene Lamont grew testy discussing the subject.

"We weren't trying to walk him," Lamont said. "Don't get me wrong, our pitchers don't want Mark McGwire to hit home runs off them, but they want him to have a legitimate chance to set the record. But they're not going to go out there and say, 'Here, knock the heck out of it,'"

McGwire's fifth homer in four days electrified a sellout crowd of 45,082—only the Pirates' second of the season—that gave him standing ovations with every at-bat and booed when Cordova walked him in the third inning.

"Oh, yeah, you can feel it," McGwire said. "It takes me off guard when you hear it on the road. I don't think any visiting player is used to playing before different crowds, all of them cheering for you."

McGwire nearly hit his 53rd in the seventh inning, bringing the flashbulb-popping crowd out of their seats again as center fielder Adrian Brown ran down his long drive a few feet short of the wall. McGwire went 2-for-3, hitting a single ahead of Ray Lankford's homer in the fifth.

McGwire's chase of the most famous individual record in sports overshadowed Pittsburgh's sixth straight victory, even in the Pirates' own ballpark. There were louder cheers for McGwire's towering homer—only his second in two seasons against the Pirates—than for Kevin Young's two-run double in the first or Cordova's unexpected RBI triple in the second.

Lamont got so many questions about McGwire's homer—and so few about the Pirates' big night—that he finally asked reporters, "Doesn't anybody want to talk about what we did?"

But it was a McGwire homer that the crowd wanted—and a McGwire homer they got.

The fans, thousands of whom filled usually empty seats two hours before gametime, were clearly disappointed when the Cardinals didn't take batting practice following back-to-back doubleheaders in New York. McGwire homered in his first 11 batting practice swings yesterday.

But McGwire didn't wait long to hit one for real. He fouled off Cordova's first pitch, swung through a changeup on the second, then hit a McGwiresque shot to right-center.

"That was by accident, believe me," McGwire said of his opposite-field shot. "I wasn't sure if I'd hit it hard enough. Last weekend, I was guessing against him too much, so I just tried to react to the ball."

Fans in sold out Three Rivers Stadium cheer Mark McGwire's first-inning home run against the Pirates in Pittsburgh, August 22. (AP/Wide World Photos—Gary Tremontina)

AUGUST 22

ANDRO

By STEVE WILSTEIN
AP Sports Writer

Sitting on the top shelf of Mark McGwire's locker, next to a can of Popeye spinach and packs of sugarless gum, is a brown bottle labeled Andros-tenedione.

For more than a year, McGwire says, he has been using the testoster-one-producing pill, which is perfectly legal in baseball but banned in the NFL, Olympics and the NCAA.

No one suggests that McGwire wouldn't be closing in on Roger Maris' home run record without the over-the-counter drug. After all, he hit 49 homers without it as a rookie in 1987, and more than 50 each of the past two seasons.

But the drug's ability to raise levels of the male hormone, which builds lean muscle mass and promotes recovery after injury, is seen outside baseball as cheating and potentially dangerous.

"Everything I've done is natural. Everybody that I know in the game of baseball uses the same stuff I use," said McGwire, who also takes the popular muscle-builder Creatine, an amino acid powder.

Sammy Sosa, close to McGwire in the homer chase, uses Creatine after games to keep up his weight and strength. For energy before games he takes the Chinese herb ginseng.

"I think Creatine is getting a bad rap now because people abuse it," McGwire said. "That's the problem. It says to take one to two scoops a day.

"People started taking 15 or 20. If you abuse anything you're going to hurt yourself."

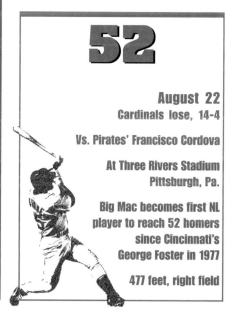

52

August 22
Cardinals lose, 14-4

Vs. Pirates' Francisco Cordova

At Three Rivers Stadium
Pittsburgh, Pa.

Big Mac becomes first NL player to reach 52 homers since Cincinnati's George Foster in 1977

477 feet, right field

AUGUST 23

SOSA STAYS CLOSE

By RICK GANO
AP Sports Writer

CHICAGO (AP)—Sammy Sosa's not hung up on racing Mark McGwire or chasing Roger Maris. At least that's what he says.

But his forceful swing, one that looks like it could rip his rib cage apart when he misses, tells a different story.

"I'm not going to lie to you. Lately, I've been swinging a little bit out of control. I was impatient the last couple of days," Sosa said Sunday after hitting his 50th and 51st homers for the Chicago Cubs in a 13-3 loss to the Houston Astros.

"People see the way I swing but it is the same. The only thing I did I was more relaxed and tried to make contact. When I try to pull everything, I get out of control. I told myself to slow down and be patient," Sosa said.

Sosa's 51 homers are the second-most in the club history and left him trailing St. Louis' Mark McGwire by two in the race to overtake Roger Maris' 61. McGwire hit his 53rd today in Pittsburgh.

The Cubs' club and NL record is 56 homers by Hack Wilson in 1930.

"We are trying to make the playoffs and Mark's trying to break the record. I got my money on Mark," Sosa said. "He's the type who can hit five or six in two days."

The hype surrounding the homer race is not bothering Sosa. He's still joking, laughing and enjoying the incessant notoriety.

"I'm still having a good time and tonight I'm going to go home and have a couple of glasses of wine with my wife," he said. "I still have 30-some games left. Let's see what happens."

Both of Sosa's homers carried far over Wrigley Field's ivy-covered walls but they couldn't carry the Cubs to victory on a day when the wind was blowing out at 16 mph.

Sosa had gone nine at-bats since his last homer Friday when he drove a 3-2 pitch from Houston's Jose Lima completely over the bleachers in left-center field and onto Waveland Avenue in the fifth inning.

The drive, that cut Houston's lead to 4-2, was estimated at 440 feet.

With a crowd of 38,714 at Wrigley Field standing and chanting his name, Sosa stepped out of the dugout for a curtain call.

That was about all the fans had to cheer about until Sosa came to bat again in the eighth. Then he hit a 1-0 pitch from Lima deep into the left-field bleachers.

Sosa hit a changeup for his first homer, a fastball for the second.

"I enjoyed the first homer myself," Lima said. "I'm not the only one to give up a homer to Sammy Sosa. The second one I said 'up, up' in the air and then I forgot it's Wrigley Field. If I struck him out, I'd enjoy it, too. But we got the win."

Ausmus said the Astros went right at Sosa and the score of the game was no factor in pitch selection.

"We're not going to pitch around a guy when we have a 10-run lead or a even a five-run lead when he's pursuing a record like that, especially a heralded one," Ausmus said.

The Cubs got a run in the bottom of the fourth on singles by Brant Brown and Tyler Houston and a check-swing RBI grounder from Gary Gaetti. Sosa's homer made it 4-2 in the fifth.

sideNOTE

Sammy Sosa's 50th and 51st homers mark just the second time two National League hitters have had 50 homers in the same season. In 1947, Ralph Kiner of Pittsburgh and the New York Giants' Johnny Mize tied for the league lead with 51 each.

Mireya Sosa admires a painting of her son Sammy Sosa in her home in San Pedro de Macoris, Dominican Republic. Sosa bought this modest house for his mother last year on Mother's Day and she has adorned the walls with baseball memorabilia of her son. (AP/Wide World Photos—Milton Gonzalez)

PROUD MAMA

By R.B. FALLSTROM
AP Sports Writer

ST. LOUIS (AP) — "My son will get as many home runs as God wants," Sammy Sosa's mother said after watching Mark McGwire edge closer to breaking the major league home-run record Monday. Mireya Sosa said from her home in the Dominican Republic that she is optimistic her son still could pass McGwire to set a new home-run record.

"What I know is that my son will get as many home runs as God wants, not one more or one less," she said. "What is happening this year to Samuel is because of the prayers that I say every day."

Mireya Sosa's home in San Pedro de Macoris, about 40 miles east of Santo Domingo, has frequently been packed with visitors watching this season's games.

The home run race has dominated Dominican newspapers and television for weeks. The country's newspapers have featured the Sosa-McGwire showdown on a daily basis.

53

August 23
Cardinals lose, 4-3

Vs. Pirates' Ricardo Rincon

At Three Rivers Stadium
Pittsburgh, Pa.

Big Mac's 111th homer over last two seasons, most ever by a righthanded batter in consecutive years

393 feet, left field

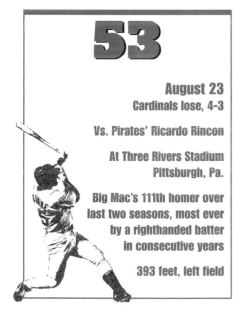

50

August 23
Cubs lose, 13-3

Vs. Astros' Jose Lima

At Wrigley Field
Chicago, Ill.

Sammy becomes the second Cubs player to hit 50 home runs in a season, joining Hack Wilson who hit 56 in 1930

440 feet, left field

51

August 23
Cubs lose, 13-3

Vs. Astros' Jose Lima

At Wrigley Field
Chicago, Ill.

Sosa's ninth multi-homer game of 1998

380 feet, left field

AUGUST 1998

ON THE ROAD TO 61

By STEVE WILSTEIN
AP Sports Writer

ON THE ROAD TO 61 (AP)—
Then there was the shot that ...

Flew higher than the left field foul pole in Coors Field, over Madeline's ice cream shop, bounced a few feet from a startled couple sitting on a bench licking cones, then into the parking lot, past the players' fancy cars, and crashed against the fence near the railroad tracks, oh, about 700 feet from home plate.

The crowd, 20,000 showing up two hours early for batting practice, surged to watch, mouths agape. If the fence weren't there and the ball hopped a freight train rumbling by, why, it might have traveled over the Rocky Mountains.

So grows the legend of Mark McGwire as Roger Maris and 61 loom ever closer.

Then there was Sammy Sosa's drive, the one that ...

Flared low through the wind blowing in at Candlestick, soared up, up, up over metal bleachers where no one hits them, not a fence-scraper like his first of the night, special delivery near the Priority Mail sign in dead center, 480 feet on the fly, tying him for a day with McGwire at 46. McGwire would pull ahead the next day, then Sosa would tie him again at 47.

And how about Ken Griffey Jr.'s dinger that ...

Crashed hard into the blue tarp in center at the Kingdome, a tidy 396-foot liner that gave him 41 through July, triggered the Mariners' typically extravagant fireworks, and left vapors and hope hanging in the air that he would be the anointed one to break the record.

Is Griffey going, going, gone from the chase? Surely he's capable of catching fire again, ripping 10 homers by the end of the month, making this a fluid three-way race once more, with maybe all of them passing Maris.

Or maybe none will do it. Maybe Maris' mark, already older than Babe Ruth's record from 1927 to 1961, will withstand another assault as it did last year when McGwire smacked 58 and Griffey 56.

How cool is this season-long home run derby? So cool that even a perfect-game pitcher like the New York Yankees' David Wells, a man who so reveres baseball history he wears Babe Ruth's cap, would get a thrill in helping them break the record.

"We're watching history in the making," Wells said. "I love it. I wouldn't want to lose a game, but if I were on the mound with a 10-0 lead against one of them when they had 61, I'd groove one just to see them whack the ball and break the record. Then I could be the answer to a trivia question."

Ruthian is baseball's ultimate adjective. McGwiresque may someday surpass it. What McGwire does ought to count for an extra run, like a 3-pointer in basketball.

McGwire's shots are flying over lighted palm trees in San Diego, over rock gardens, evergreens and fountains in Denver, over Big Mac Land in St. Louis, busting seats and signs, beyond walls and imagination.

"For sheer, awesome distance, no one I know who has ever played the game has hit balls so far, so consistently," says San Francisco manager Dusty Baker, who played with a fellow named Aaron. "Big Mac has hit the longest balls in just about every park in the majors."

Yet, there is only disdain in McGwire's tourmaline green eyes for the mammoth batting-practice blows, meaningless, he knows. He feels like the big monkey of the moment, performing in a cage.

Everyone's analyzing his every move, every word, every new silver hair in his red goatee.

"My goal is to get through this season without my beard turning all gray," McGwire says, knowing people will use those flecks as evidence of pressure—the same kind that made Maris' hair fall out.

They watch McGwire stretching like a yogi before games, meditating in poses, his body remarkably supple for one who is 6-foot-5, 245 pounds with forearms twice as thick as the barrel of his bat. Sosa and Griffey are powerfully built, but on a smaller scale.

"Sammy's a little bigger version of Mickey Mantle or Willie Mays," says Chicago Cubs manager Jim Riggleman. "He doesn't hit a lot of huge homers. If it scrapes the back of the wall going out, it counts the same as if it goes up in the third deck. Henry Aaron didn't hit prodigious home runs. The outfielder ran to the wall thinking he had a chance. I'd take 755 of those over 100 that go 500 feet."

So would McGwire or anyone else. But there's something breathlessly exciting about watching a ball launched off McGwire's bat.

"Americans love power," McGwire says. "Big cars. Big trucks. Big people. Baseball fans have always been drawn to the home run and the guy throwing close to 100 mph. That's what they want to come and see.

"I remember as a kid I always wanted to go see Mike Schmidt or Dave Kingman, or Nolan Ryan and Frank Tanana. It's like going to see golfers, John Daly when he came in and was hitting over 300, then Tiger. Not everybody can do that."

In every ballpark, fans wear his No. 25. In St. Louis, there is a red sea of No. 25 jerseys, "McGwire" on the backs of thousands. When he comes in from the field to sign autographs before batting practice, the sea swells like a giant wave toward him, kids imploring, "Please, Mr. McGwire," adults sometimes knocking kids out of the way, shoving all kinds of stuff at him to sign.

On the road, McGwire checks into hotels under a pseudonym to avoid intrusive calls and knocks. He's claustrophobic, hates tight spaces, feels cornered in small crowds and elevators. Even at dinners with his son, devouring steak after steak, strangers come up to him, sit down, want to chat and get his autograph.

Some meteorological observers say he and Griffey and Sosa are hitting so many homers because it's been such a hot, sticky summer. The way these guys swing, they could hit snowballs 400 feet in January.

McGwire's power comes from more than his 20-inch biceps. He's blessed with uncanny timing and hand-eye coordination, and helped by contacts that improve his vision from 20-500 to 20-15 in each eye. He's developed a knack for hitting the ball just under the center to give

it enough backspin to ride the air. A short, compact, quick swing generates enormous bat speed.

But the biggest mechanical change he's made in recent years is to release the bat with his right hand just after contact, giving him full extension and even more distance.

Nobody, especially McGwire, puts much credence in the accurate-sounding distances announced in different ballparks. They're all estimates, even the ones based on computer programs that take into account whether the ball was a high-arcing drive, a liner, or somewhere in between, and where it would have landed on a level field.

A homer in May in St. Louis, where a giant Band-Aid on a sign in center marks the spot, is supposedly his farthest—545 feet. But that's just a guess, though it's probably more accurate than the supposed 565-foot homer Mickey Mantle was said to have hit in 1953.

"Not many people would be here if he weren't hitting them so darned long," said Jeff Wahl, one of the thousands packing the left field stands during batting practice recently in Denver. "I mean, quit hitting 500-foot home runs and people will stop coming out. Batting prac-

tice isn't baseball, but it's still fun to watch."

Sosa is always loose, the kind of guy who carries on a conversation between swings, in Spanish and English. Where McGwire stands utterly still, bat on shoulder, in deep meditation before batting, Sosa can't stop moving.

He takes practice swings with his big black bat and black gloves, stretches one way then the other, looks around for family and friends in the crowd from his home in the Dominican Republic.

Sosa insists McGwire's still The Man and he's just another kid.

He says he's not swinging for homers even when he's swinging from the heels. He gulps ginseng for energy before games, chugs beer to chill out afterward.

Something must be working. Another 20-homer month like June and he'll blow away Maris and Ruth, and probably McGwire and everyone else.

Many of those homers don't go much farther than the first few rows of the bleachers, but they count the same as McGwire's gargantuan drives.

"It's not how far, it's how many," Dusty Baker said.

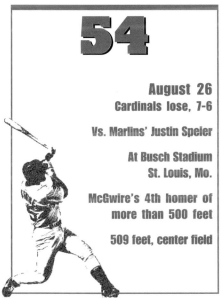

54

August 26
Cardinals lose, 7-6

Vs. Marlins' Justin Speier

At Busch Stadium
St. Louis, Mo.

McGwire's 4th homer of more than 500 feet

509 feet, center field

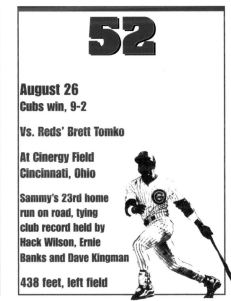

52

August 26
Cubs win, 9-2

Vs. Reds' Brett Tomko

At Cinergy Field
Cincinnati, Ohio

Sammy's 23rd home run on road, tying club record held by Hack Wilson, Ernie Banks and Dave Kingman

438 feet, left field

53

August 28
Cubs win, 10-5

Vs. Rockies' John Thomson

At Coors Field
Denver, Colo.

Sammy pulls to within one homer of Big Mac

414 feet, right field

AUGUST 29

McGWIRE EJECTED

By R.B. FALLSTROM
AP Sports Writer

ST. LOUIS (AP)—Mark McGwire was ejected for arguing a questionable called third strike in the first inning of St. Louis' game against Atlanta, missing a chance to add to his total of 54 home runs and drawing a noisy demonstration from a sellout crowd at Busch Stadium.

McGwire, 4-for-27 against Atlanta this year (.148) with just one homer and one RBI, became incensed after getting called out on a low 3-2 pitch on the inside part of the plate. At one point he fought his way around third-base coach Rene Lachemann, who was trying to act as a shield.

After a foul ball by Atlanta's Ryan Klesko on the first pitch of the second inning, a fan, at the urging of those around him, heaved the ball back on the field. Other fans followed by tossing debris on the field and then chanted "We want Mac!, We want Mac!," halting the game for about 10 minutes.

Ushers lined the field during the delay, and were later joined by police officers to prevent further disturbances.

Joe Walsh, the Cardinals' director of security, said a few fans had been escorted from their seats but that the team was more interested in calming everybody down. The team called in police to help return the situation to normal.

"You can understand the emotions when 48,000-plus are here to see one guy," Walsh said. "This was definitely a tense situation."

It was McGwire's first ejection since he joined the Cardinals July 31, 1997.

AUGUST 30

BIG MAC BLASTS NO. 55

By R.B. FALLSTROM
AP Sports Writer

ST. LOUIS (AP) — Mark McGwire swears it's just coincidence the way he keeps trumping Sammy Sosa.

Hours after Sosa connected for his 54th home run, McGwire hit No. 55 to regain the major-league lead in an 8-7 victory over the Atlanta Braves. His last three homers have come on the same day as Sosa has homered.

But no, the St. Louis Cardinals' slugger insisted, there was no extra incentive.

"I've said this time and time again," McGwire said. "I only can take care of Mark McGwire, period."

McGwire said his three-run, 501-foot shot in the seventh inning was special mostly because it capped the Cardinals' comeback from an early six-run deficit.

"They always feel good," he said. "But it even feels better when you win a ballgame the way we did against if not the best, one of the best teams in the National League."

McGwire, who is within one of tying Hack Wilson's NL record, has 26 games remaining to break Roger Maris' record of 61 homers in 1961. Fifteen of those games are at Busch Stadium, where he has hit 29 homers to obliterate the previous record of 17.

McGwire's first homer in four games came on 1-0 pitch from Dennis Martinez (3-6) and disappeared over the backdrop beyond the center-field wall. It was his fifth 500-foot-plus homer at Busch this season and the crowd of 44,051 demanded—and got—a curtain call.

"That was a bomb," Martinez said. "That wasn't the first one I've given up and it won't be the last. Good for him."

Mark McGwire and Atlanta Braves pitcher Dennis Martinez watch Big Mac's 55th home run of the season sail out of Busch Stadium, August 30, in St. Louis. (AP/ Wide World Photos—John Gaps III)

55

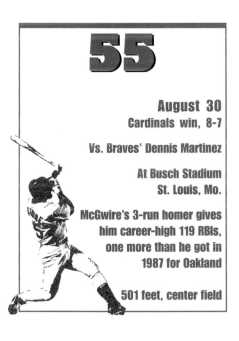

August 30
Cardinals win, 8-7

Vs. Braves' Dennis Martinez

At Busch Stadium
St. Louis, Mo.

McGwire's 3-run homer gives him career-high 119 RBIs, one more than he got in 1987 for Oakland

501 feet, center field

54

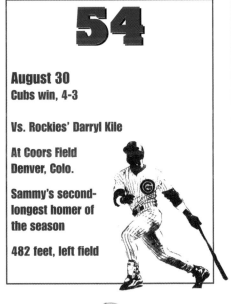

August 30
Cubs win, 4-3

Vs. Rockies' Darryl Kile

At Coors Field
Denver, Colo.

Sammy's second-longest homer of the season

482 feet, left field

55

August 31
Cubs win, 5-4

Vs. Reds' Brett Tomko

At Wrigley Field
Chicago, Ill.

Eighteenth time this season McGwire and Sosa have homered on same day

364 feet, left field

SEPTEMBER 1

BIG MAC PASSES HACK

By STEVEN WINE
AP Sports Writer

"This is a great thing happening in baseball. We don't know if it'll ever happen again."

— Mark McGwire

MIAMI (AP) — As Mark McGwire stepped to the plate in the ninth inning, more than a dozen youngsters scrambled onto a banked tarp beyond the center-field wall, eager to catch some history.

It came their way moments later, a baseball launched an estimated 472 feet, giving McGwire a National League record with 57 home runs this season.

The homer was McGwire's second of the night. He broke Hack Wilson's record of 56 homers set in 1930, leading the St. Louis Cardinals over the Florida Marlins 7-1.

"I've never seen anything like it," said Marlins manager Jim Leyland, who has been in professional baseball since 1964. "The guy is hitting balls out of Yellowstone Park."

"It's a pretty awesome feat," McGwire agreed. "I'm totally excited."

The Cardinals slugger pulled ahead of Sammy Sosa, who remained at 55 homers. With 24 games remaining, McGwire is on pace to hit 67 home runs. Roger Maris' major league record is 61.

"Now it's getting a little bit exciting," Sosa said after his Chicago Cubs beat Cincinnati 6-5. "Mark has 57 and that's a lot. Everybody knows that everybody is pulling for Mark, and I'm pulling for Mark, too. And I want him to break the record first."

McGwire's latest power surge came after he flied out in the first inning, drew playful boos for hitting a mere single in the third, and grounded out in the fifth.

McGwire laughed when fans playfully booed him for hitting a mere single in the third inning. "I started to think, 'I hope they understand that this is not an easy task,'" McGwire said.

Leading off the seventh, he homered on a 1-1 fastball from Livan Hernandez, sending the pitch an estimated 450 feet over the center-field wall.

Even McGwire was impressed with the trajectory.

"It hung up there so long, I wondered if it was ever going to come down," he said. Two innings later, he hit the first pitch from Donn Pall to almost the same spot. Each homer prompted a standing ovation from the crowd of 37,014 and a curtain call from McGwire.

Pall said McGwire connected on a split-finger fastball.

"I don't want to be part of history," Pall said. "It means nothing to me. I don't care what number it is. I'll hold my head up high because I went after him with my best stuff."

"Two curtain calls is an unbelievable feeling for an athlete," McGwire said. "It means a lot."

Both homers sailed over the head of center fielder Todd Dunwoody.

"It looks like he hits with a golf club, he makes the ball look so small," Dunwoody said.

The balls were recovered by a Little League outfielder and a teenage magician, who gave the souvenirs to McGwire in exchange for autographed balls, bats, jerseys, photos and tickets to tonight's game.

"The stuff is better than the money," said Jason Duncan, 11, who retrieved homer No. 56. "It was a hard decision to make, but I knew it meant a lot to him."

Michael Pitt, a high-school senior and part-time magician, recovered No. 57.

"I called off work tonight," he said. "I said to my friends, 'I'm going to catch a Mark McGwire ball.' I don't even think they believed that I was going to the game because I'm the class clown, so nobody believes me."

It was McGwire's seventh multihomer game this season and the 50th of his career.

"It's a magical moment, what's happening with him and Sammy," said the Marlins' Hernandez (10-11). "All you could do was watch it and be part of the moment."

Mark McGwire slugs his 57th home run of the season against the Florida Marlins, breaking Hack Wilson's 68-year-old National League record. (AP/Wide World Photos—John Gaps III)

Wilson's NL record of 56 homers was set in 1930 for the Chicago Cubs. He also had 190 RBIs that season, still the major league record. McGwire has driven in 121 runs.

Before his latest homers, McGwire was batting just .222 this season against the Marlins, who have the worst pitching staff in the league. But McGwire hit a 545-footer, his longest of the season, against Hernandez in St. Louis on May 16.

"Two home runs, one mile," Hernandez joked. The Marlins' right-hander has allowed 31 homers this season—third-most in the NL.

Almost forgotten was a fine performance by Matt Morris (5-4), who allowed one run in seven innings. Ron Gant hit his 22nd homer and Ray Lankford added his 25th for the Cardinals.

But it was the McGwire homers that dazzled everyone—even his manager.

"Mark continues to amaze," Tony La Russa said. "What he's doing is impossible to describe."

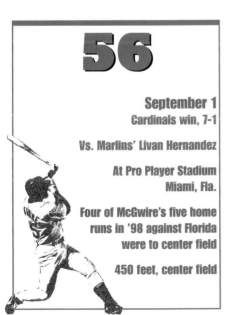

56

September 1
Cardinals win, 7-1

Vs. Marlins' Livan Hernandez

At Pro Player Stadium
Miami, Fla.

Four of McGwire's five home runs in '98 against Florida were to center field

450 feet, center field

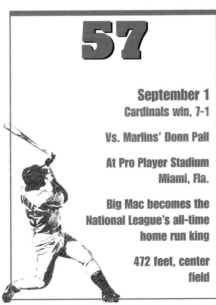

57

September 1
Cardinals win, 7-1

Vs. Marlins' Donn Pall

At Pro Player Stadium
Miami, Fla.

Big Mac becomes the National League's all-time home run king

472 feet, center field

SEPTEMBER 2

SOSA'S 56TH TIES CUBS RECORD

By RICK GANO
AP Sports Writer

"People will now remember two guys, Hack Wilson and myself."
— Sammy Sosa, after hitting his 56th home run to tie Wilson's 68-year-old Cubs and National League record

56

September 2
Cubs win, 4-2

Vs. Reds' Jason Bere

At Wrigley Field Chicago, Ill.

Sammy's record-tying blast also helps Cubs set a club-record with homers in 15 straight games

363 feet, right field

CHICAGO (AP) — Sammy Sosa knows a little about Hack Wilson and his incredible season of 1930. There is even a picture of the former Chicago Cubs outfielder resting on the wall near Sosa's locker.

Now Sosa has a share of the mark Wilson held alone for those 68 years—the team record with 56 home runs.

Nice, says Sammy. But the way he sees it, there is no reason to stop now, especially with Mark McGwire, Roger Maris and even bigger records still there to chase.

"Fifty seven is a lot and everybody knows that. Mark has the possibility to come back tonight and hit two more. He's playing in Miami don't forget," Sosa predicted just hours before McGwire did just that, hitting his 58th and 59th to go three up on Sosa and move within two of Roger Maris' long-standing record.

"I know a little about Hack because his picture is next to my locker," Sosa said when he hit his 56th homer.

"He was a great player when he was playing. He drove in 190 runs, and that is a lot. I am lucky to be there at the right time. And the season is not over yet."

Sosa hit a solo homer in the sixth off Cincinnati's Jason Bere, and the Cubs beat the Reds 4-2, thanks to Gary Gaetti's two-run homer in the eighth.

But the outcome, as always, was overshadowed by another historic homer.

"The record is there for somebody to break. Whatever I do this year or in the future, somebody will break my record, too," Sosa said.

Earlier in the season, while still with the Chicago White Sox, Bere surrendered a homer to McGwire in interleague play.

"They've hit a ton between them," he said. "You just hope it's not at a point in the game that really hurts you."

Sosa's homer into the first row of the right-field seats gave the Cubs a 1-0 lead and charged the crowd. Fans chanted for a curtain call, and as usual he gave them what they wanted.

The homer was Sosa's 15th to right field this season, and this one just made it.

"Those count, too," Bere said.

"I would have liked to have gotten the ball down, but I elevated a little and he took it the other way. He didn't try to do anything else with it other than go the other way, and he has enough power that he can hit it out to all fields."

With runners on first and second and two outs in the seventh, Sosa flied out to left against John Hudek to complete a 2-for-4 day that also included a ground out and a bad-hop single.

The Cubs, 16 games over .500 for the first time since 1989, lead the Mets by one game for the NL wild card. After Gaetti's 14th homer made it 3-2, Scott Servais hit his seventh homer to give the Cubs a two-run cushion.

"It's incredible to be able to do what Sammy and Mark are doing," said Gaetti, who played with McGwire and the Cardinals earlier in the season. "They are kind of feeding off each other. I'm in a unique situation to see both sides. ... I got to root for Sammy. When he hits home runs, we're going to win."

REMEMBERING HACK

By MARIO FOX
AP Writer

CHICAGO (AP)—It happened before expansion teams. Before minor-league pitchers were throwing in the majors. Before the squeezed strike zone.

Before all that, there was Hack Wilson and his splendid season.

In 1930, the Chicago Cubs slugger drove in 190 runs, still the major league record, and hit 56 homers, still the National League high.

In 1930, Babe Ruth was in his prime. The baseball season was packed with offense, blamed on a juiced ball. Wilson's amazing summer—he also had a .356 batting average and a .723 slugging percentage—earned him a place in the Hall of Fame in 1979.

Another Hall of Famer, Billy Williams, doesn't think Wilson's RBI total will ever be matched.

"So many things have to happen. Guys have to get on base and you have to drive them in. It's just impossibly hard to get 190," said Williams, now a Cubs coach.

As the years passed, Wilson's mark has become harder to reach. Lou Gehrig's 184 for the Yankees in 1931 is still the second-highest season RBI total. The last player to come close to Wilson was Tommy Davis of the Los Angeles Dodgers with 153 in 1962. Ralph Kiner came closest to the NL homer run mark, with 54 in 1949 for Pittsburgh.

Wilson was quite a sight—195 pounds on a 5-foot-6 frame. He had an 18-inch collar, size 6 shoes and swung a 40-ounce bat he called "Big Bertha."

Wilson batted cleanup, loved high fastballs and was a capable center fielder. A right-hander, he

Hack Wilson

seldom pulled the ball; his power was to right and right center.

Off the field, Wilson was known as a brawler and boozer. Former Chicago White Sox owner Bill Veeck, who started in baseball working for his father, Cubs president William Veeck, told of finding Wilson in the clubhouse before a game, sitting in a tub of water beside a huge block of ice while the trainer tried to sober him up.

He was born Lewis Robert Wilson on April 26, 1900, and there are two stories about how he came to be called Hack. Some say it was because he resembled Cubs player Hack Miller. Others point to a wrestler of the day named Hackenschmidt, whom he also resembled.

Wilson's career took off after an inauspicious beginning with the New York Giants. Demoted to Toledo, he was picked up by the Cubs for $5,000 in a 1926 minor-league draft. It was a bargain. He hit over .300 with at least 21 home runs for the next four seasons. The 1930 Cubs had a team batting average of .309, with five starters hitting .335 or better.

By June 5 of that summer, Wilson had 17 homers and 52 RBIs. His RBI total climbed to 74 on July 1, 106 on Aug. 1 and 158 on Sept. 1. He hit his 50th homer on Sept. 15.

The Cubs were in and out of first place much of the season, but they finished second to the St. Louis Cardinals. On Sept. 28, the last day of the season, Wilson hit his 56th homer and drove in four runs.

His production fell sharply after 1930, and his major league career lasted only a few more seasons. After retiring in 1935 he played on some barnstorming teams, drank a lot, divorced, remarried and held a variety of jobs.

Wilson quit his heavy drinking late in life, but his health was ruined. He died at age 48 on Nov. 23, 1948, in Baltimore, three months after Ruth died. His body lay unclaimed for three days, but the National League office wired $350 to pay for the funeral, according to Gerald Grunska, co-author of *Hack*.

In one of his last interviews, Wilson said his drinking problems began during that epic 1930 season.

"I received a salary of $40,000. I started to drink heavily," he said. "I had a lot of natural talent ... but I sure lacked a lot of other things, like humility and common sense."

BIG MAC HEADS HOME WITH 59

By STEVEN WINE
AP Sports Writer

"It's amazing. You can't throw the guy any pitch he can reach or he hits it 500 feet. It's a little unfair at times. He's like the Michael Jordan of baseball. He's unreal."
— Florida pitcher Rob Stanifer

MIAMI (AP)—Mark McGwire is going home to St. Louis with 59 homers and four new souvenirs.

McGwire hit two homers for the second consecutive night against the Florida Marlins, giving him a career-high 59. He needs just two more to tie Roger Maris' 37-year-old major league record.

McGwire homered in the seventh inning against Brian Edmondson and again in the eighth on the first pitch from Rob Stanifer. Each was a two-run shot.

The first, which landed halfway up in the upper deck in left field, was estimated at 497 feet, making it the third-longest in the history of Pro Player Stadium. His second homer 30 minutes later was to left-center and traveled an estimated 458 feet, giving the St. Louis Cardinals a 14-3 lead.

It was McGwire's eighth multihomer game this season and the 51st of his career. With 23 games remaining, he's on a 69-homer pace, and his recent charge—12 homers in 15 days—gives him a shot at 70.

Maris hit 61 homers in 1961.

"I didn't expect to have 57 by September 1," McGwire said before the game, "but when I got to 50, I began to think about the record."

His 58th came hours after Sammy Sosa hit No. 56 for the Chicago Cubs.

"Sammy's a September player, so you have to watch out for him," McGwire said. "It's crunch time—time to make history."

McGwire broke Hack Wilson's 68-year-old NL record of 56 home runs with two yesterday.

The Cardinals slugger surpassed his career best of 58 homers last year—34 for Oakland and 24 for St. Louis. The only players to hit more home runs in a season were Maris and Babe Ruth, who hit 60 in 1927. Ruth hit 59 in 1921.

Now it's three to go to break Maris' record. The only other player ahead of McGwire is Babe Ruth, who hit 60 homers in 1927. Ruth also hit 59 in 1921.

"Quite amazing, isn't it?" McGwire said. "What's going on now is pretty big."

The Cardinals begin a three-game series Sept. 4 at home against Cincinnati, but McGwire declined to speculate about his chances of breaking the record this weekend.

"I'll do my best," he said. "Let's not look so far ahead and just take what today has given us."

McGwire has surpassed Ruth's major-league record of 114 homers in consecutive seasons, set in 1927-28.

McGwire homered on a 2-1 pitch in the seventh, giving the Cardinals a 9-0 lead. The homer came after McGwire hit into a double play and walked twice in his previous plate appearances.

Even McGwire was impressed by his first homer. He golfed a 2-1 pitch from Edmondson that was low and inside, then pumped his right first as he trotted toward first base.

"The pitch was probably three inches off the ground," McGwire said. "I amazed myself that I went down and got it."

"It'd be scary to see what he

Mark McGwire—59 and counting. (AP/Wide World Photos—Leon Algee)

could do with a set of golf clubs," Edmondson said.

The standing ovation from the crowd of 45,170 lasted for about a minute, prompting a curtain call by the Cardinals slugger. There was another curtain call an inning later.

When McGwire stepped to the plate again in the eighth, catcher Randy Knorr was still shaking his head about the homer.

"How did you hit that pitch?" Knorr asked.

"I have no idea," McGwire said. Then jumped on a first-pitch slider from Stanifer into the seats in left-center. After that, manager Tony La Russa took McGwire out of the game, and the crowd booed, then headed for the exits.

The game also attracted more than 400 media, the largest following yet for McGwire's home-run chase.

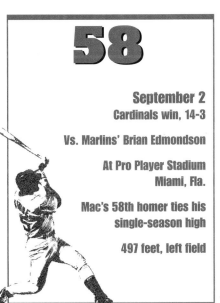

58

September 2
Cardinals win, 14-3

Vs. Marlins' Brian Edmondson

At Pro Player Stadium
Miami, Fla.

Mac's 58th homer ties his
single-season high

497 feet, left field

59

September 2
Cardinals win, 14-3

Vs. Marlins' Rob Stanifer

At Pro Player Stadium
Miami, Fla.

McGwire sets mark for most
home runs ever by a right-
handed hitter

458 feet, left field

SOSA SETS CUBS RECORD

By ALAN ROBINSON
AP Sports Writer

"Talk to me September 28th."
—Sammy Sosa, after being asked how many home runs he will hit in 1998.

57

September 4
Cubs win, 5-2

Vs. Pirates' Jason Schmidt

At Three Rivers Stadium Pittsburgh, Pa.

Sammy's fifth homer in six games sets a Cubs club record

374 feet, right field

PITTSBURGH (AP)—Sammy Sosa collected a piece of history by hitting his 57th home run, then sprinted into the Chicago Cubs clubhouse to do what the rest of America was doing.

He wanted to watch Mark McGwire.

Reporters crowded around his tiny stall in the Three Rivers Stadium visitors clubhouse, and boom microphones hovered overhead to pick up his every word. But McGwire was batting, so Sosa wasn't talking.

Finally, McGwire struck out to go 0-for-3 and delay history for at least one more day, and Sosa was ready to talk about breaking a home run record that had stood for 68 years.

No, not that record. Roger Maris' mark of 61 homers in 1961 held up for one more day, even if it might not last until Labor Day now that McGwire has 59 and Sosa has 57.

But Sosa's first-inning solo homer off a now-dented outfield scoreboard in the Cubs' 5-2 victory over Pittsburgh did break Hack Wilson's club record of 56 homers in 1930. Sosa wonders if his record will stand nearly that long.

"After I retire, my name will be there for a long time," Sosa said. "We got the win. I got the home run. I got the record. That's something there."

Sure, McGwire has 12 homers in the last 18 days, but Sosa has

eight in 12 games. And Sosa's 48 homers in his last 88 games might be unequaled in major league history.

And if McGwire should happen to go into a slump just when he seems on the verge of ...

"No, Mark McGwire is on a different level than me," said Sosa, who had never hit more than 40 homers until this season. "He's Superman. I'm just another kid on the block. I'll never say I want to go up there and beat Mark. I just hope to finish strong."

He already is. Before Sosa hit his fifth homer in six games, he predicted McGwire would finish with 70 homers.

He only hopes the Cubs are still playing. With 21 games remaining, they have won five straight and eight of nine to maintain their one-game lead over New York in the NL wild-card race. They also handed the Pirates their seventh straight loss.

"I just want to make the playoffs, that will make this season that much better," Sosa said.

Even if it seemingly can't get much better than this. Sosa needed only three pitches to put even more pressure on McGwire, lining Jason Schmidt's 2-0 fastball off the right-field auxiliary scoreboard in the first inning.

The crowd of 36,510, many of whom were lured away from the opening night of high school football, gave him a thunderous ovation

Cubs slugger Sammy Sosa is usually surrounded by autograph seekers wherever he goes. (AP/Wide World Photos—John Gaps III)

HOT TIX

By NATALIE GOTT
Associated Press Writer

ST. LOUIS (AP)—Ryan Record would give his savings to be in the stands when St. Louis Cardinals slugger Mark McGwire hits his 62nd home run.

"I'd give $400 or $500," Record, 24, said while standing in the ticket line at Busch Stadium Thursday, desperately hoping to get a ticket for a weekend game. "If he was sitting on 61, I'd pay a lot. I'm that much of a fan."

McGwire hit two home runs Wednesday night against the Florida Marlins, giving him 59, only three short of breaking Roger Maris' 1961 record of 61. So anticipation is high that McGwire will break the record during the Cardinals' five-game homestand against the Cincinnati Reds and the Chicago Cubs.

Fans in baseball-mad St. Louis are lining the streets, tying up phone lines and surfing the Internet to find tickets to the games.

At the stadium ticket window, they asked repeatedly, "Do you have any tickets left for Saturday?" "Anything left in left field?" "What about Friday, anything left for Friday?" All the ticket sellers could do was answer no.

The Cardinals are virtually sold out for their final 14 home dates at Busch Stadium and have projected a season attendance of 3.2 million.

"I tried calling all day yesterday and all morning long before I gave up and just drove down here," said Richard Palmer, sighing as he realized that between the Cardinals' home game schedule and his work schedule, the only game he could attend would be September 24 against the Montreal Expos.

By then, Palmer said, McGwire probably will have broken the record. But he didn't fret long. He bought seven tickets. "At least I got left field," Palmer said. "You can't beat that."

that rated a curtain call. Until McGwire—there's the name again—homered twice in two days August 22-23, that had never happened to a visiting player in Pittsburgh.

Sosa scored the Cubs' first two runs—he singled in the fourth and scored on Jose Hernandez's grounder—then drove in the go-ahead run in a three-run ninth inning after Schmidt was lifted.

Sosa was credited with an RBI when third baseman Freddy Garcia couldn't handle his hard-hit grounder, and Mark Grace followed

with a two-run single off Jason Christiansen.

Gary Gaetti, Sosa's teammate, could say he's never seen anything like it, but he'd be lying. He spent most of season with McGwire and the Cardinals before joining the Cubs, so he's been an eyewitness to home run history.

McGwire. Sosa. McGwire. Sosa.

"You just shake your head. I've seen most of Mark McGwire's, and I haven't seen as many of Sammy's, but I know he's helping us win games, and that's what I like the best," he said.

SEPTEMBER 5

BIG MAC MEETS THE BABE

By BEN WALKER
AP Baseball Writer

"Wake up, Babe Ruth! There's company coming!"
—Veteran Cardinals broadcaster Jack Buck, calling Mark McGwire's 60th home run

ST. LOUIS (AP)—With a Ruthian shot, Mark McGwire met the Babe.

McGwire was watching the whole way, taking a wide turn while his eyes followed the flight of the ball he launched today. And when that high-arching drive landed in the left-field seats, home run No. 60 was his.

McGwire became just the third player to hit so many, tying Ruth's mark and moving within one homer of Roger Maris' record total.

"To be compared with Babe Ruth is just awesome," McGwire said.

"Until recently, I never thought anything like that could happen."

It didn't take McGwire long to do it—either in this game or this season.

A night after appearing anxious at the plate, McGwire connected for a two-run shot in the first inning against Cincinnati rookie Dennis Reyes. Fireworks exploded over Busch Stadium and McGwire saluted the sellout crowd of 47,994 with a curtain call.

The home run came in the Cardinals' 142nd game, including a tie.

Ruth hit No. 60 on the final day of a 154-game season in 1927, and Maris hit No. 61 on the last day of a 162-game schedule in 1961.

Now, McGwire has 21 games left to beat Maris and hold off Sammy Sosa, who hit his 58th in the Chicago Cubs' game Saturday night at Pittsburgh.

McGwire struck out swinging in his other three at-bats, his feet often flying off the ground because of his big cuts, in a 7-0 win over the Reds. Each time he came to the plate, everyone in the ballpark was ready. Several Reds players sprung to the top step of the dugout when he batted, leaning on the rail to get a better view.

McGwire's home run came on a 2-0, low-and-in fastball from Reyes.

"Like I said yesterday, if he's going to get me, he's going to get my best pitch," Reyes said. "When he hit the ball, I knew it was out."

An afternoon that began with Cardinals Hall of Famer Stan Musial playing "Take Me Out to the Ballgame" on his harmonica near home plate quickly turned into McGwire's day. Even Musial admitted that when he asked his grandchildren to name their favorite player, they answered, "Mark."

At 381 feet, McGwire's homer was not one of his longer ones, but its height and the way he watched it was reminiscent of the kind made famous by Ruth, who died 50 years ago.

The souvenir was caught by Deni Allen, 22, who works in the St. Louis Rams' marketing department.

Allen agreed to give the ball to McGwire. In return, the Cardinals said they will give him two season tickets for 1999, some bats, hats and autographed balls, plus a round of batting practice before a game at Busch later this season.

Mark McGwire watches his 60th home run of the season leave the park at Busch Stadium against Cincinnati Reds pitcher Dennis Reyes, September 5. (AP/Wide World Photos—Amy Sancetta)

58

September 5
Cubs win, 8-4

Vs. Pirates' Sean Lawrence

At Three Rivers Stadium
Pittsburgh, Pa.

Sammy climbs to tie for fourth on major league baseball's all-time list

417 feet, right field

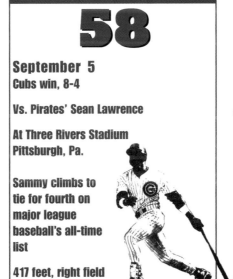

60

September 5
Cardinals win, 7-0

Vs. Reds' Dennis Reyes

At Busch Stadium
St. Louis, Mo.

Big Mac ties The Bambino's 60 in just 142 games

381 feet, left field

BIG MAC TIES MARIS WITH NO. 61

By PAUL NEWBERRY
AP Sports Writer

"When he grabbed his son, that was a great moment. Anyone who has kids knows what it's like to go play ball with your kids."
—Cubs catcher Scott Servais, the father of three children

ST. LOUIS (AP)—Mark McGwire took his place alongside Roger Maris today, tying one of baseball's most hallowed records with home run No. 61.

The landmark drive came in the first inning against the Chicago Cubs, on just the third pitch thrown to McGwire by Mike Morgan.

Meantime, Chicago's very own home run hero, Sammy Sosa—just behind McGwire with 58—smiled and clapped in appreciation.

The crowd cheered wildly as McGwire held both arms wide and high as he approached first base and got a high five from the Cubs' Mark Grace.

Waiting at home plate was McGwire's 10-year-old batboy son, Matt, who had arrived from California only minutes before Dad made history. The slugger hoisted the youngster in his massive arms and gave him a bear hug.

McGwire nodded his appreciation to the standing, roaring crowd, and then sent a special signal to members of the Maris family seated on the first-base side: He pointed his right index finger to the sky, tapped his heart three times and blew them a kiss.

"He tapped his heart, like dad was in his heart," said Kevin Maris, a son of the Yankees slugger.

Indeed, that was the message: "I know he's with me and that's really all I can say—thank you to all the Marises," McGwire said. "I admire everything that Roger went through because I know what he went through now. I am very, very happy to be linked with him."

McGwire's drive slammed off the facade of the stadium club—the third deck at Busch Stadium—and fell into the packed stands below.

Mike Davidson, a 28-year-old from St. Louis, wound up with it after it deflected off the hands of three other people.

The lucky fan said he planned to give the ball to McGwire and wouldn't ask for anything in return.

On the same field where Maris played his final game in 1968, McGwire's sense of timing was impeccable, as usual. He had his son in the dugout, his father in the stands on his 61st birthday, his biggest rival applauding the moment from right field.

"I've hit 61, Mark. I don't know why you shouldn't be able to do it," John McGwire told his son when the two had dinner the night before.

It didn't take long. In the first inning, McGwire launched Mike Morgan's fastball inside the left-field foul pole, the ball slamming off the third-deck facade some 430 feet away, setting off a wild scene below when it deflected back into the crowd.

After the 61st homer, former teammate Gary Gaetti high-fived McGwire as he was making the final turn toward home.

On the last step of his trot, McGwire hopped on the plate with both feet for emphasis.

When Sosa came to the plate in the top half of the first, the crowd—clad mostly in Cardinal red—saluted the Cubs' slugger with a standing ovation, quite a tribute considering the longstanding rivalry between the teams.

Sosa tipped his hat to the crowd and gave his trademark two-finger salute to McGwire, holding a runner at first.

The crowd wasn't as loud when McGwire, batting third in the

Mark McGwire gets a hug from his father, John, after the game which saw Mark tie Roger Maris' major league home run record of 61 home runs, September 7. John McGwire was celebrating his 61st birthday. (AP/Wide World Photos—Eric Draper)

Cardinals order, stepped up in the bottom of the inning with two outs. Out in right field, Sosa clapped his right hand against his glove.

Three pitches later, the scene turned into bedlam. After missing the first pitch and taking a ball, McGwire sent the ball hurtling toward the left-field stands. A day earlier, a McGwire drive had taken a similar path but hooked foul by about 7 feet. This time, there was no doubt.

Tomorrow night will likely be McGwire's last realistic chance to break the record at home. The Cardinals leave on a five-game road trip, and McGwire's longest stretch without a homer is 29 at-bats.

"Like I have said probably 100,000 times, I can only take care of myself, try to get a ball to hit, and get a good swing on it," McGwire said. "But I'm going to give it my best shot."

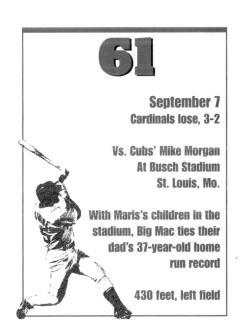

61

September 7
Cardinals lose, 3-2

Vs. Cubs' Mike Morgan
At Busch Stadium
St. Louis, Mo.

With Maris's children in the stadium, Big Mac ties their dad's 37-year-old home run record

430 feet, left field

NO. 62!

By BEN WALKER
AP Baseball Writer

ST. LOUIS (AP)—He did it with a rocket shot to left that barely cleared the wall.

No magical moonshots. No stately arcs.

Baseball history was expected from Mark McGwire since the day he arrived at spring training. On a late summer night he delivered.

McGwire hit his 62nd home run, winning the race to break Roger Maris' 37-year-old record and doing it without a doubt or an asterisk—and with plenty of games to spare.

It was McGwire's shortest home run of the season—341 feet—but it still gave him the biggest, most glamorous record in sports.

"I have been talking about this since January," he said. "I can honestly say I did it."

McGwire connected with two outs in the fourth inning off the Chicago Cubs' Steve Trachsel for the historic homer, which punctuated the chase that he began with a grand slam on opening day.

When it finally happened, McGwire was so caught up in the moment that he missed first base as he rounded the bag and had to return to touch it, pulled back by coach Dave McKay.

"I sort of missed one big thing — to touch first base," he said. "I hope I didn't act foolish, but this is history."

From there, McGwire got handshakes from every Chicago infielder

as he trotted home and then hugged catcher Scott Servais.

McGwire was mobbed by his teammates at home plate, where he hoisted his 10-year-old batboy son Matt high into the air. McGwire then ran into the seats to hug the family of Maris, whose record he had just broken.

Before the game, McGwire held the bat that Maris used to hit his 61st and rubbed it against his chest.

"Roger, I hope you're with me tonight," McGwire said.

He was, indeed.

Cubs right fielder Sammy Sosa, who has 58 home runs, ran in from

> "He is the only person walking the face of the Earth who could do what he did, and he belongs to us."
> — Cardinals broadcaster Jack Buck, addressing a crowd of fans at a rally on Sept. 9, on Mark McGwire

right field to hug McGwire. They bashed their arms together, and McGwire gave Sosa a mock punch to the stomach. Sosa reciprocated with his trademark: kissing his fingers, tapping his heart, holding up his fingers in a V in honor for the late Harry Caray, an announcer who worked for the Cardinals and Cubs.

As the specially marked ball cleared the left-field fence, there was no scramble to retrieve it because it landed in an area where no fan could get it.

Tim Forneris, a ground-crew worker, picked it up and later gave

it to McGwire in a postgame party on the field. McGwire also got a '62 red Corvette from the Cardinals in the tribute and he and his son took a slow victory drive around the field as the crowd cheered.

"Right when it hit off the bat, I knew it was going out and it went right over the sign," Forneris said. "There was a bunch of ground-crew guys on the wall. But I was right on the edge and I said, 'That ball is mine.'"

By tomorrow, that landmark ball, along with McGwire's bat and jersey, will be on display at the Hall of Fame in Cooperstown, N.Y.

The homer triggered an 11-minute delay, baseball's biggest midgame celebration since Cal Ripken broke Lou Gehrig's consecutive games record in 1995.

After McGwire finished celebrating with his teammates and the Maris family, he grabbed a microphone to address the sellout crowd of 43,688, which was still standing and cheering.

"To all my family, my son, the Cubs, Sammy Sosa. It's unbelievable," McGwire said. "Thank you, St. Louis."

McGwire, who appeared anxious in grounding out on a 3-0 pitch in the first inning, hit his solo shot on the first pitch, an 88 mph fastball at 8:18 p.m. CDT.

"I was hoping it wasn't going to be me," Trachsel said.

The home run, despite its short distance, surely will rank as one of the biggest in history, up there with the ones hit by Bobby Thomson, Bill Mazeroski, Hank Aaron, Carlton Fisk, Kirk Gibson and Joe Carter.

"I couldn't be happier for him," Roger Maris Jr. said.

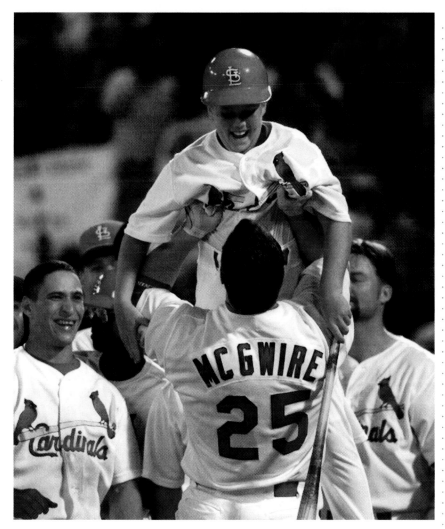

Mark McGwire lifts his son Matthew at home plate after hitting his record-setting 62nd single-season home run off Chicago Cubs pitcher Steve Trachsel in the fourth inning, September 8, in St. Louis. (AP/Wide World Photos—Ed Reinke)

BALL NO. 62

By TED ANTHONY
AP National Writer

ST. LOUIS (AP)—When homer No. 62 finally came, the whole affair proved far easier than anybody thought.

The talk had flowed everywhere for weeks. Who'd catch it? Should they keep it? Would the IRS come calling?

And the most pressing question: Give it back gratis or take Mark McGwire and the Cardinals for as much cash and cool stuff as possible?

Unlike so many of McGwire's home runs, this one didn't make it into the left-field stands. Instead, the line drive shot over the left field fence, where Tim Forneris—part of the Busch Stadium ground crew—ran it down and picked it up.

He promptly set about returning the specially and secretly marked, individually numbered ball to The Man Of The Hour.

At a postgame ceremony, Forneris presented McGwire with the ball.

"Mr. McGwire, I think I have something that belongs to you," he said.

62

September 8
Cardinals win, 6-3

Vs. Cubs' Steve Trachsel

At Busch Stadium
St. Louis, Mo.

Sports' most glorious record now belongs to Big Mac

341 feet, left field

SEPTEMBER 9

BASEBALL'S REACTION TO NO. 62

By RONALD BLUM
AP Sports Writer

When Mark McGwire hit his 62nd homer, the crowd noise reverberated throughout baseball.

In Philadelphia, Phillies manager Terry Francona could tell from the crowd noise at Veterans Stadium.

"I heard the fans making noise and I thought it must have happened," he said. "I thought it was kind of neat that so many people had radios and that they cared about McGwire. It's just great for the game."

At Fenway Park in Boston, both the Yankees and the Red Sox marveled.

"Just an amazing feat, right up there with Joe DiMaggio's hitting streak," Yankees pitcher David Cone said.

Cal Ripken of the Baltimore Orioles knows a little bit about what Mark McGwire was feeling.

"It was very heartwarming for me to sit there and watch it, and watch the emotion, the interaction between him and his parents, between him and his kid," Ripken said after McGwire's 62nd homer broke Roger Maris' record. "It brings a certain amount of humanity to the event."

Around the major leagues, players watched the historic homer on clubhouse televisions.

"Pretty cool, wasn't it?" Atlanta's Greg Maddux said. "You just want to congratulate him and

pray he hits none off you next year."

At Comiskey Park in Chicago, players could tell McGwire broke the record from the noise of fans

> "He might be the best of all time."
> — Frank Thomas of the Chicago White Sox on Mark McGwire

cheering in the Bullpen Sports Bar behind right field.

"It gives you goose bumps," said Frank Thomas, a two-time AL MVP. "He's always been the best home-run hitter I've ever seen. It couldn't happen to a better person. To hit 62 home runs in one season is unheard of"

Players were excited at the attention McGwire has drawn to baseball, still recovering from the 1994-95 strike.

"He's made a fan of the world," Houston's Craig Biggio said.

Biggio's teammate Jeff Bagwell said what made the record extra

special was that the home-run watch began for McGwire even before opening day.

"From day one, before day one, Mark McGwire was supposed to get this record," Bagwell said. "To know that everyone wanted him to hit home runs and then go out and do it, that's awesome."

The Oakland Athletics had fond thoughts for their former teammate, traded to St. Louis on July 31, 1997.

"That's the happiest he's ever been," Jason Giambi said. "We were in the clubhouse watching. It's exciting to be able to call Mac my friend. We were tight here and still keep in touch. I still feel a big part of it."

In Oakland, the Cardinals game was shown on the stadium videoboard during batting practice.

"Literally, chills went down the back of your neck and your spine," Minnesota's Paul Molitor said. "Almost everybody was fixated on the big screen."

Joe Carter, who hit the winning homer in the 1992 World Series for Toronto, also was thinking about McGwire.

"You can get lucky one time, but not 62," he said. "I have no idea what that feels like to do that. To come through in a situation like that, every single day everything is scrutinized, every at-bat. I can't fathom to think what it felt like."

Cardinal slugger Mark McGwire reacts to receiving the ball he hit for his record-breaking 62nd home run of the season from grounds crew worker Tim Forneris, right, as Roger Maris Jr., center, and Kevin Maris look on, at a postgame ceremoney in St. Louis, September 8. (AP/ Wide World Photos—Ed Reinke)

THE DAY AFTER NO. 62

By JOE KAY
AP Sports Writer

CINCINNATI (AP)—No sleep. No day off. No home runs.

The day after Mark McGwire hit No. 62, it took a Ruthian effort just to stay awake and please a crowd that came to cheer baseball's new home run king.

A sleepless McGwire got another incredible ovation from a record crowd tonight, then kept his eyes open long enough to go 0-for-2 in a 6-3 loss to the Cincinnati Reds.

He didn't add to his record, but he added to his growing lore by choosing to play when he needed to rest. When he came to the plate in the first inning, there was magic.

He backed away three times and waved as the crowd gave him a stand-ing ovation that lasted for more than a minute.

McGwire was touched.

"I tipped my hat and I was ready to hit and it got louder and I backed off and looked and Pete was tipping his cap," McGwire said. "Taubensee said some great things that went right to my heart. What a great feeling!"

Before nodding off, he gave the 51,969 fans—the largest weekday crowd in stadium history except for season openers—something to photograph and remember.

The St. Louis Cardinals didn't get into town until 4:30 a.m. because of the Busch Stadium celebration of McGwire's 62nd homer last night. When he finally got to his hotel room, McGwire couldn't sleep because history was play-ing out in his mind.

McGwire batted twice—he grounded out and flew out—before leav-ing the game. He tossed a ball and both batting gloves to fans behind the Cardi-nals dugout before heading for the club-house.

"I think people want to see McGwire in person," Reds manager Jack McKeon said. "If he hits one, fine. If he doesn't hit one, so what? They want to come out and see him.

"I'd love to see Babe Ruth play, even if he didn't hit one, just so I could say I saw Babe Ruth play. I think it's the same scenario here."

SOSA JOINS THE 60-SOMETHING CLUB

By RICK GANO
AP Sports Writer

CHICAGO (AP)—Sammy Sosa joined the 60-something club. What an exclusive one it is.

Before this month, only two players—Babe Ruth and Roger Maris—had reached 60 homers in a season this century. Now Sosa and Mark McGwire have done it in an eight-day span.

"I just have to say that I could never feel more happy than I do today," a smiling Sosa said after he hit his 60th homer and his team, the Chicago Cubs, rallied with five ninth-inning runs for a wild 15-12 win over the Milwaukee Brewers.

Nearly an hour after the game had ended on Orlando Merced's dramatic three-run, pinch-hit homer, hundreds of fans stayed in their seats at Wrigley Field, hoping for a another glimpse of Sosa, who with Michael Jordan pondering retirement, is the most popular man in the city.

And as he emerged from the dugout after an interview session, they began chanting his name again. He waved.

Sosa, now tied with the legendary Ruth, who hit 60 homers in 1927, is one shy of the 61 hit by Maris in 1961. And he trails contemporary and good friend McGwire by two after the St. Louis slugger failed to homer in Houston.

"Babe Ruth was one of the greatest guys to play baseball," Sosa said. "He never really died. He's still alive. Everybody remembers him like it was yesterday. It's great to be tied with the Babe and be be-hind Roger Maris and Mark."

Sosa drove a seventh-inning pitch from Milwaukee Brewers reliever Valerio De Los Santos over the back fence and out of Wrigley Field.

The 430-foot blast ended up on the front steps of a house across the street from the park. The three-run homer cut Milwaukee's lead to 12-7 after the Brewers had forged a 10-2 lead following an eight-run third inning.

"We had second and third and I didn't want to strike out," said Sosa, who fought off several pitches. "I came through. I hit 60, I jumped up and said 'Yes,' and that was about it. I didn't want to show the other team up."

Sosa, who went 2-for-3 with two walks, gave the crowd of 39,170 what they came to see. They were already on their feet when his line drive to left took off—there was never a doubt where it was headed.

The crowd went bonkers, standing and cheering and chanting his name until the man who once sold fruit and shined shoes on the dusty streets of his native Dominican Republic came out for a thunderous curtain call.

"Sammy's homer just lifted us, it gave us hope," Cubs manager Jim Riggleman said. "This is probably the sweetest win I've ever been involved with, if the not the strangest."

59

September 11
Cubs lose, 13-11

Vs. Brewers' Bill Pulsipher

At Wrigley Field
Chicago, Ill.

Sosa's first homer in a Cub loss since Aug. 23

464 feet, right field

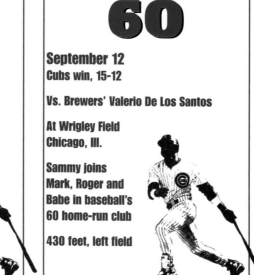

60

September 12
Cubs win, 15-12

Vs. Brewers' Valerio De Los Santos

At Wrigley Field
Chicago, Ill.

Sammy joins Mark, Roger and Babe in baseball's 60 home-run club

430 feet, left field

STANDING ALONE AT THE TOP

By R.B. FALLSTROM
AP Sports Writer

ST. LOUIS (AP)—He started with a home run in his very first Little League at-bat. Years later, when he reached the majors, he set a home run record for rookies.

He won a World Series title as one of the "Bash Brothers" and has revitalized his sport, his bulging biceps headlining the news each night during the summerlong pursuit of Roger Maris' record.

And now, with his 62nd homer Tuesday night, Mark McGwire stands alone at the top of baseball.

Hard to believe he didn't think much of himself as a Little Leaguer.

"I started playing when I was 9," McGwire said. "Was I any good? I guess I was pretty good, but I don't think I was that good."

Nobody—but nobody—would believe that. The evidence of greatness is all over Mark David McGwire's life, and his conquering of Maris' home run record is just the culmination.

McGwire seemed linked with home runs from the start: He was born October 1, 1963—two years to the day after Maris hit No. 61. And McGwire hit his 61st home run on the day his father, John McGwire, turned 61.

At Southern California, McGwire set the Pacific-10 Conference record for home runs in a season with 32. He was an important part of the 1984 U.S. Olympic team. And when he played his first full season in the major leagues in 1987, he was already a finished product.

"When he first started in Oak-land, we had no one fundamentally better than Mark McGwire," La Russa said.

McGwire set a rookie record with 49 home runs that year, a total that took him nine seasons to top. He drove in 118 runs, a total he didn't top until this season.

McGwire, who'll turn 35 in October, could reach 500 homers next season and write his ticket to the Hall of Fame.

The only reason he has just 449 is a series of back and heel problems that robbed him of most of the 1993 and '94 seasons and cast doubt on his durability.

The first baseman has produced several seasons' worth of highlights, toppling milestones with almost every long ball:

• He matched Willie Mays' 1971 record when he homered in each of the first four games of the season.

• In May, he surpassed Babe Ruth by reaching 400 homers in the fewest at-bats.

• It only took him until early June to set the Busch Stadium season home run record with his 18th. On July 26, he smashed Johnny Mize's team record of 43 homers.

His home runs at Busch Stadium became so commonplace that fans felt cheated if he didn't hit one. They certainly weren't much for sticking around if it didn't look good, with hundreds racing for the exits after what appeared to be his final at-bat of the day.

"It's amazing. The people get out of there and go get drinks and cool off and wait for him to come up again. I'd probably do the same if I could," said the Cardinals' Matt Morris.

Also watching for many of the games this summer was his 10-year-old son, Matthew, the Cardinals' batboy at home games. Matthew was just 1 when McGwire and his wife, Kathy, divorced.

All year, McGwire downplayed his chances of breaking baseball's most cherished record—until he got to home run No. 50.

When he got there ridiculously early, on August 20, even McGwire had trouble not getting giddy about the whole thing.

Teammates along for the historic ride grinned, too. McGwire's chase has reduced the Cardinals' sub-.500 season to a mere footnote.

"The guy is doing it all by himself," La Russa said. "He's got tremendous support, but he doesn't need it. He's a self-contained phenomenon."

McGwire reached September with 55 home runs, and the hits just kept coming. The major casualty during that burst was Hack Wilson's 1930 NL record of 56 home runs.

So where does all this wind up? Now that he has the record, does he hold it? Does he break it again in 1999?

"I think McGwire is going to chase it next year," Canseco said. "He is incredible."

SEPTEMBER 13

SOSA TIES MARIS, McGWIRE IN SAME DAY

By RICK GANO
AP Sports Writer

CHICAGO (AP)—Not so fast, Mark. Slammin' Sammy may win the race for the home run record after all.

Sammy Sosa tied Mark McGwire on Sunday, connecting twice against the Milwaukee Brewers to raise his total to 62.

"It's unbelievable. It was something that even I can't believe I was doing," Sosa said following the Cubs' 11-10, 10-inning victory. "It can happen to two people, Mark and I."

For his part, McGwire went 0-for-2 against the Astros in Houston before leaving the game in the fourth inning with minor back spasms. He is just 1-for-14 since breaking Roger Maris' record with home run No. 62 last Tuesday against the Cubs in St. Louis.

"It's awesome, outstanding," McGwire said of Sosa. "I've been doing this for the last few years with Ken Griffey. We go back and forth.

"We've got until the 27th of September. I don't think you have to be a rocket scientist to figure out it's not over. I never once thought that was it."

Sosa, who trailed McGwire 24-9 in late May, homered off Bronswell Patrick in the fifth inning, sending an 0-1 pitch 480 feet into the street behind the left-field fence at Wrigley Field. Sosa hit an-

other 480-foot homer in the ninth, a solo shot off Eric Plunk.

That one dropped Babe Ruth into fourth place on the single-season list with 60, which he hit in 1927. Roger Maris hit 61 homers in 1961 for a record that McGwire

> "I don't usually cry, but I cry inside. I was blowing kisses to my mother, I was crying a little bit."
> —Sammy Sosa, after hitting home runs No. 61 & 62

broke Tuesday against the Cubs in St. Louis.

Now, amazingly, a mark that had stood for 37 years has been passed twice in less than a week.

With tears and sweat running down his face as he sat in the dugout after his second triumphant tour around the bases, Sosa came out for three emotional curtain calls. Fans littered the field with paper cups and other debris while

chanting "Sam-mee! Sam-mee!" causing a delay that lasted six minutes.

"I have to say what I did is for the people of Chicago, for America, for my mother, for my wife, my kids and the people I have around me. My team. It was an emotional moment," Sosa said.

In Sosa's hometown of San Pedro de Macoris, where his mother watched the game, residents flooded into the streets to celebrate. It was there that Sosa once shined shoes and sold oranges to help support his family.

Sosa, who has four homers in his last three games, was carried off the field after the victory, which kept the Cubs one game ahead of the New York Mets in the NL wild-card race. He was on deck when Mark Grace hit the game-winning homer.

"I thought pretty much the home run race was going to be McGwire's," Grace said. "But when my buddy gets hot, he can hit them in a hurry. And he proved that.

"I just hope Sammy gets the attention he deserves. Not only has he hit 62 homers, but he has carried us. He is without a doubt the MVP of the National League."

Sosa said that when he saw the response McGwire got from hometown fans for homer No. 62, he wanted to make sure he was in Chicago when he matched it.

Both of Sosa's homers cleared the back fence at Wrigley Field, sending fans scrambling for balls worth tens of thousands of dollars to memorabilia collectors.

After the first homer, a parade of fans raced after the ball as it went down the street. Sosa, meanwhile, rounded the bases pumping his fists as the sellout crowd began stamping its feet.

By the time Sosa struck out in the seventh, the street was filled with fans. When he hit in the ninth with the Cubs trailing 10-8, they were chanting "62! 62!"—and Sosa didn't disappoint them.

Cubs slugger Sammy Sosa is carried on the shoulders of his teammates at the end of a game in which he hit his 61st and 62nd home runs, September 13. (AP/Wide World Photos—Beth A. Keiser)

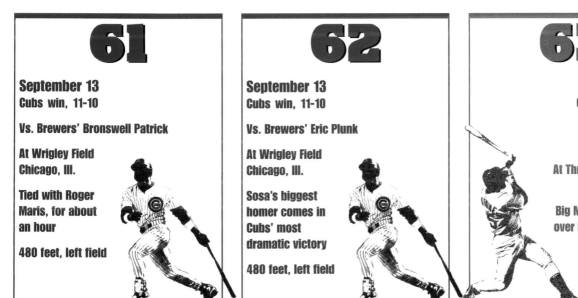

61

September 13
Cubs win, 11-10

Vs. Brewers' Bronswell Patrick

At Wrigley Field
Chicago, Ill.

Tied with Roger Maris, for about an hour

480 feet, left field

62

September 13
Cubs win, 11-10

Vs. Brewers' Eric Plunk

At Wrigley Field
Chicago, Ill.

Sosa's biggest homer comes in Cubs' most dramatic victory

480 feet, left field

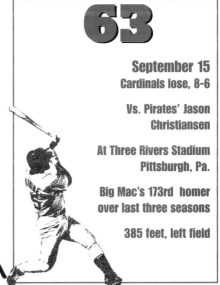

63

September 15
Cardinals lose, 8-6

Vs. Pirates' Jason Christiansen

At Three Rivers Stadium
Pittsburgh, Pa.

Big Mac's 173rd homer over last three seasons

385 feet, left field

SEPTEMBER 16

63 FOR SAMMY

By BERNIE WILSON
AP Sports Writer

SAN DIEGO (AP)—Slammin' Sammy evened the home run race again, fittingly, with a grand slam.

With a mighty swing at a dramatic moment, Sammy Sosa hit his 63rd homer to a place balls rarely go at Qualcomm Stadium, the second deck in left field. Just like that, after struggling for two games, Sosa pulled back into a tie with Mark McGwire in the greatest home run derby ever.

"It was something exciting, I have to say, especially with the game on the line," Sosa said after driving in all his team's runs in the Chicago Cubs' 6-3 win over the San Diego Padres.

Or with two outs and the scored tied 2-2. In that situation, he said, he didn't want to strike out. Instead, he continued to make history.

With cameras flashing from all around the stadium and most of the crowd of 49,891 on its feet, Sosa drove a 93 mph fastball from Brian Boehringer an estimated 434 feet.

The crowd went wild when Sosa's ball settled inside the foul pole, setting off a mad scramble for the souvenir, and Sosa was summoned back onto the field for a curtain call.

The cheering continued after the inning ended, and Sosa doffed his cap to the crowd when he went to right field.

"People are excited about the home run race, and rightfully so," winning pitcher Terry Mulholland said. "There's no telling if they'll ever see it again."

Sosa and McGwire, tied for the most home runs in a season, each have nine games left. Sosa said he didn't care who wins the thrilling race for the single-season homer record.

"I got to the point that everybody wanted me to go, and whatever happens from now on is a gift," said Sosa. "Now I want to go to the playoffs."

Sosa, who hit a two-run, bases-loaded double in the seventh, helped the Cubs hold their half-game lead over New York in the NL wild-card race.

Fabian Perez Mercado, 32, of Tijuana, Mexico, ended up with Sosa's home run ball. He was at the game with his pregnant wife and two children.

Sosa tied McGwire at 62 on September 13 when he connected twice in a stunning performance at Wrigley Field. That gave him four homers in three days.

McGwire went back ahead when he hit his 63rd when he pinch-hit for the Cardinals in ninth inning of the first game of a double-header last night.

The historic home run race has fostered goodwill throughout baseball, except, it seems, in the Padres' clubhouse.

"Don't get me wrong, everybody in this clubhouse loves Sammy," Greg Vaughn said. "But how are we supposed to take it? What happens when they leave town on tomorrow? Are we supposed just to take them (the fans) back with open arms?"

Sosa finished 3-for-5 with six RBIs as Chicago won its second in a row and fourth in five games. He had been 1-for-9 with six strikeouts in the first two games of the series.

Sosa tied a career high with six RBIs in a game, and took over the major league lead with 154 RBIs this season, the highest total in the National League since Joe Medwick in 1937.

63

September 16
Cubs win, 6-3

Vs. Padres' Brian Boehringer

At Qualcomm Stadium
San Diego, Calif.

Sosa's third grand slam among his last 24 homers

434 feet, left field

64

September 18
Cardinals win, 5-2

Vs. Brewers' Rafel Roque

At County Stadium
Milwaukee, Wisc.

Big Mac's 10th homer against Brewers pitchers in 1998

417 feet, left field

CELEBRATING SAMMY

By NANCY ARMOUR
AP Sports Writer

CHICAGO (AP)—Sammy Sosa got a new convertible, a painting and a crystal statue. His adoring fans got another magical moment to remember.

As the ceremony to celebrate his amazing year ended today, Sosa took off on a victory trot around Wrigley Field. With the theme from "Superman" blaring over the loud-speakers, he waved his cap to the fans, many of whom were bowing and chanting "M-V-P! M-V-P!"

"That run just showed the fans I love them very much," Sosa said after the game. "I'm real proud of myself and real happy the fans showed me their appreciation to-day."

The game wasn't nearly as much fun for Sosa as his party. He didn't homer—he went 0-for-5 and is now 0-for-17 since hitting a grand slam Wednesday—and remains at 63, two behind Mark McGwire of the St. Louis Cardinals.

His mother and siblings were there from the Dominican Republic. So was Juan Marichal, the Hall of Fame pitcher who is now the Secretary of Sports in the Dominican Republic. Baseball Commissioner Bud Selig and Roger Maris' children also were present.

One look around Wrigley Field showed this was definitely Sosa's day. A huge sign in left field read, "Sammy: YOU'RE the Man." The team pennants that usually fly above Wrigley were gone, replaced by Dominican flags and pennants with "Sosa" on one side and "21" on the other.

Chicago's Sammy Sosa receives the Commissioner's Historic Achievement Award from Baseball Commissioner Bud Selig during Sammy Sosa Day festivities at Wrigley Field, September 20. Sosa's son, Sammy Jr., applauds his dad on the field. (AP/Wide World Photos—Michael S. Green)

Sosa's family got front-row seats for the ceremony, though that wasn't good enough for his son, Sammy Jr. As soon as the little boy saw his father and Selig walk up to the microphone, he broke free of the family and ran to Sosa.

Selig started off the gift-giving, presenting Sosa with the Commissioner's Historic Achievement Award. McGwire sent a letter of congratulations.

But the best gift might have been the new, maroon Plymouth Prowler convertible. As Sosa looked over at the car in right field, a huge grin crossed his face. Not bad for a boy who grew up selling oranges and shining shoes to help support his family.

"It's been something special," Sosa said. "Thank you very much and God bless all of you."

BIG MAC TURNS 65

By ARNIE STAPLETON
AP Sports Writer

MATT'S PREDICTION: 65

By R.B. FALLSTROM
AP Sports Writer

ST. LOUIS (AP) — Having achieved the lofty home run goal his 10-year-old son set for him this spring, Mark McGwire now tries to see if he can top it.

The St. Louis Cardinals slugger has six games left, all at home, to build on his major league record of 65 homers and try to hold off Sammy Sosa.

No. 65 was special for McGwire because that was the number Matthew McGwire, the Cardinals' batboy whenever he's in town, had forecast for his father before spring training.

"That's all I thought about when I was running around the bases," McGwire said Sunday. "That ball means a lot to me. I hope I get it back."

MILWAUKEE (AP)—Michael Chapes feels he was deprived of a piece of history, and he has no doubt Mark McGwire was robbed, too.

Chapes caught the ball that would have been home run No. 66 had second-base umpire Bob Davidson not ruled fan interference.

The ball was quickly snatched from Chapes' mitt, and when the 31-year-old high school gym teacher protested to security officials, he got no sympathy, a $518 fine for interfering with a ball in play and a police escort out of County Stadium.

"It was definitely a home run," Chapes said. "This whole thing makes me sick."

McGwire knows the feeling.

"After further review, it looked like it was a home run," McGwire said. "The man who caught the ball, he never came across the yellow line."

McGwire hit No. 65 in the first inning to extend his record in the St. Louis Cardinals' 11-6 victory over the Milwaukee Brewers. But the day was tainted by the debatable call.

Cardinals manager Tony La Russa said the club is appealing to the National League to make the unprecedented move of reversing the umpire's call and awarding the homer after the fact.

"They asked us to look at it, and that's all I can say right now," NL spokeswoman Katy Feeney said at Wrigley Field, where she attended "Sammy Sosa Celebration" day.

Rule 9.02 (a) of the Official Baseball Rules states: "Any umpire's decision which involves judgment, such as, but not limited to, whether a batted ball is fair or foul, whether a pitch is a strike or a ball, or whether a runner is safe or out, is final."

Davidson, a member of the NL staff since 1983, said he couldn't be swayed by the fact the ball came off McGwire's bat.

"I could care less if he hits 150

home runs," Davidson said. "As an umpire, you can't get caught up in that."

Davidson barely had time to spin around, but swears he was in good position to make the call.

"The ball got out there in about half-a-second," he said. "I got out there as fast as I could and I saw it. When I saw it, the fan was leaning over and the ball hit him below the yellow line. So that's why I called it a ground-rule double."

McGwire moved two homers ahead of Sosa with a two-run 423-foot shot to left off Scott Karl that needed no judgment call.

McGwire would love that. He said the homer was special because his 10-year-old son, Matthew, told him in spring training that's how many he wanted his father to hit this season.

"What a prediction. My God!" McGwire said.

And what an afternoon.

Before Roger Maris set his record of 61 homers in 1961, commissioner Ford Frick declared any record would carry a "distinctive mark" if it did not beat Babe Ruth's mark of 60 in 154 games.

But now Mighty Mac has a footnote of his own. Fans will forever wonder whether his total should have been one higher.

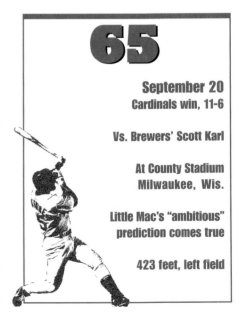

65

September 20
Cardinals win, 11-6

Vs. Brewers' Scott Karl

At County Stadium
Milwaukee, Wis.

Little Mac's "ambitious"
prediction comes true

423 feet, left field

SOSA WINS BATTLE, BUT CUBS LOSE WAR

By NANCY ARMOUR
AP Sports Writer

MILWAUKEE (AP)—Nearly an hour after the game ended, Brant Brown was still dazed as he searched for an explanation to give the reporters crowded around his locker.

It was a routine fly ball, and he felt it smack his glove for the final out. Then he felt the ball drop.

In a split-second, Sammy Sosa's slump-busting, Mark McGwire-tying two home runs were wiped out and the Chicago Cubs' playoff hopes plunged. The Milwaukee Brewers, who had trailed 7-0 earlier in the game, scored three runs on Brown's error and won 8-7.

Chicago—and Brown—caught a break when Montreal beat the New York Mets 3-0. Chicago and New York are tied in the NL wild-card race, with San Francisco $1^1/_2$ games back.

Sosa, breaking an 0-for-21 slump, hit solo shots in the fifth and sixth innings to tie McGwire at 65 and give the Cubs a 7-0 lead.

"Everybody knows what happens to me is great," Sosa said. "But at the other side, I care about winning, I care about the team and our situation right now."

At least the Cubs have Slammin' Sammy back. Sosa had been hitless since his grand slam last week in San Diego that gave him No. 63. But the Brewers, who have given up more homers to Sosa than any other team, were the perfect cure for what ailed him.

Sammy Sosa comes out of the dugout to wave to the crowd after hitting his 65th home run of the season in the sixth inning against the Milwaukee Brewers, September 23, in Milwaukee. (AP/Wide World Photos—Gary Dineen)

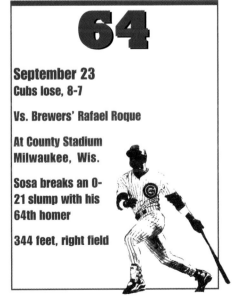

64

September 23
Cubs lose, 8-7

Vs. Brewers' Rafael Roque

At County Stadium
Milwaukee, Wis.

Sosa breaks an 0-21 slump with his 64th homer

344 feet, right field

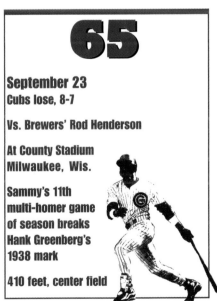

65

September 23
Cubs lose, 8-7

Vs. Brewers' Rod Henderson

At County Stadium
Milwaukee, Wis.

Sammy's 11th multi-homer game of season breaks Hank Greenberg's 1938 mark

410 feet, center field

SEPTEMBER 25

SOSA TAKES LEAD ... FOR 45 MINUTES

By MICHAEL A. LUTZ
AP Sports Writer

"Disappointed for what, man? Mark is my friend, not my enemy."
— Sammy Sosa, after a reporter told him that McGwire had hit No. 66

HOUSTON (AP)—Neither Sammy Sosa nor the Chicago Cubs wound up with the lead tonight.

Sosa hit his 66th home run, but the Cubs failed to take advantage and lost to the Houston Astros 6-2, leaving them tied for the NL wild-card spot with the New York Mets.

Sosa temporarily gained the lead in his home run race with Mark McGwire by hitting a 462-foot drive into the third level of the Astro-dome.

About 45 minutes later, however, McGwire hit his 66th in the St. Louis Cardinals' game against Montreal.

Derek Bell hit a two-run homer and Moises Alou singled home the go-ahead run in the fourth inning for the NL Central champion Astros. The Cubs lost for the fifth time in six games.

Facing friend and fellow Do-minican Jose Lima, Sosa homered leading off the fourth inning. Lima also gave up Nos. 50 and 51 to Sosa at Wrigley Field on August 23.

Shortly after Sosa's homer at the Astrodome, a fan displayed a sign saying "Sosa loves Lima."

Following Sosa's two-homer game off Lima, there was a pub-lished report questioning whether Lima grooved a pitch for the Cubs star. Both players denied the allega-tion.

Sosa had been ahead of McGwire in the home-run chase only once earlier this season. On August 19, Sosa hit No. 48 in a game against St. Louis—about an hour later, McGwire also hit his 48th and the Cardinals slugger con-nected later in the game to take the lead.

Lima (16-8) has been generous with home runs this season. He leads the team with 34 home runs allowed, fourth in the NL.

Astros starter Sean Bergman also yielded homer No. 47 to Sosa on August 16. Sosa has four against the Astros this season.

Sosa has 157 RBIs this season, fourth-most in NL history. He broke out of an 0-for-21 slump on Wednes-day with two home runs in a loss at Milwaukee.

Sosa's homer tied it at 2 in the fourth. Alou put the Astros ahead for good with his single in the bot-tom half.

September 25
Cubs lose, 6-2

Vs. Astros' Jose Lima

At The Astrodome Houston, Texas

Sosa's final homer of the regular season helps Cubs break their single-season home run record

462 feet, left field

SEPTEMBER 25

McGWIRE TIES IT UP, 66-66

By R.B. FALLSTROM
AP Sports Writer

ST. LOUIS (AP) — Take that, Sammy. Again.

Forty-five minutes after Sammy Sosa took the major league homer lead with No. 66, Mark McGwire answered with his 66th. His two-run, fifth-inning shot in St. Louis' 6-5 victory over Montreal on Friday night re-tied the home run derby with just two games to go.

Although McGwire said yet again that he didn't care who wins, his manager would be crushed if McGwire didn't finish on top.

"As far as I'm concerned, Mark's home run chase is the most important thing the next two days," Tony La Russa said. "We're pulling for him real, real, real hard."

Sosa led for 58 minutes on Aug. 19 before McGwire hit his 48th and 49th homers at Chicago. Leading off the fourth at Houston, Sosa hit No. 66 off Jose Lima, and McGwire responded with a man on and two outs in the fifth with a 375-foot drive.

"It was almost as good as 62," La Russa said.

On the first pitch from Bennett, McGwire nearly homered on a towering drive that landed just to the left of the foul pole in the upper deck in left field. Busch Stadium personnel inadvertently set off fireworks.

"False alarm," McGwire said with a grin. "The guy was trigger happy."

Expos manager Felipe Alou thought the foul drive was even more impressive than the homer.

"I've never seen a fly ball go that far in my life," Alou said. "And I've been in many different leagues." When Sosa took the lead in the home run derby, it prompted a collective groan from a sellout crowd at Busch Stadium who booed when Sosa's home run number was changed on the scoreboard.

McGwire has two homers against Montreal, and this was his first since he connected off Trey Moore on April 21. Alou suspects McGwire may hit a few more off his largely inexperienced staff.

"We don't have Greg Maddux here who can pinpoint a fastball on the corner every time," Alou said. "We have kids."

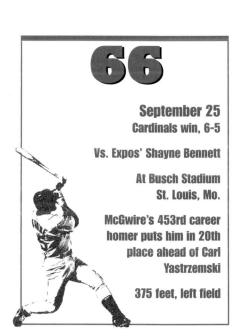

66

September 25
Cardinals win, 6-5

Vs. Expos' Shayne Bennett

At Busch Stadium
St. Louis, Mo.

McGwire's 453rd career homer puts him in 20th place ahead of Carl Yastrzemski

375 feet, left field

The scoreboard at Busch Stadium in St. Louis keeps the running home run total for Mark McGwire and Sammy Sosa after both men hit their 66th home runs September 25. (AP/Wide World Photos—Ed Reinke)

TWO AHEAD WITH ONE GAME LEFT

By R.B. FALLSTROM
AP Sports Writer

"I think Mark is trying to do exactly what he said, he's trying to take his best shot and whatever the numbers are, they are. If somebody wants to call him a failure, stand up and call it, and have your house burned, have your children kidnapped."
—Cardinals manager Tony La Russa

ST. LOUIS (AP)—Mark McGwire may have ended the great home run derby a day early. Sammy Sosa may have to settle for keeping the Cubs' postseason hopes alive.

Big Mac hit Nos. 67 and 68 in the St. Louis Cardinals' 7-6 loss to Montreal, his ninth multihomer game this season and the 52nd of his career.

"I might never let this season go. It might never happen again," McGwire said.

With one game left, McGwire is two ahead of Chicago's Slammin' Sammy Sosa and an incredible seven ahead of the record Roger Maris set in 1961.

Only one game remains in the regular season, although there's a chance Sosa's Cubs could wind up in a wild-card playoff, which would give him an extra game to catch up.

Sosa was all but conceding.

"It doesn't look good, but I still have a chance," he said after going 2-for-4 with a pair of singles in Chicago's 3-2 win at Houston. "I've always been saying Mark is going to finish ahead of me. He'll probably hit two more Sunday."

Still, McGwire is envious of Sosa.

"Obviously, it feels nice," McGwire said. "But I've got one more game, and so does he. I think he's got bigger and better things on his mind, helping the Cubs get into the playoffs."

The St. Louis Cardinals' slugger reclaimed the lead he's relin-

quished only twice all season—and then for only 103 minutes in all—hitting No. 67 off Dustin Hermanson in the fourth inning. He connected again in the seventh, a two-run, 435-shot off rookie Kirk Bullinger.

Although his actions say otherwise, McGwire said he's not in a better zone than ever.

"My focus has been pretty deep for the last two or three months," McGwire said. "I don't think it can get any deeper."

With one out in the fourth today and a sellout crowd of 48,212 on their feet and cheering, he lined a first-pitch fastball from Hermanson an estimated 403 feet into the left-field seats.

J.D. Drew doubled to chase Tim Young in the seventh and McGwire hit a 1-1 pitch from Bullinger into the left-center field bleachers, prompting a second curtain call. Fans remained standing throughout the three-run rally, which tied the game 6-all.

McGwire, who surpassed Roger Maris' former record of 61 on Sept. 8, is 1-for-3 for his career against Hermanson, who struck him out on four pitches in the first. Facing Anthony Telford in the fifth, McGwire flied out to deep center, ending the inning. He also hit a game-ending grounder off Rick DeHart, who got his first career save.

"I never dreamed it would come against Mark McGwire," DeHart said. "I'm not a closer, but my adrenaline really kicked in."

Before connecting last night, McGwire had been homerless in 14 at-bats. This time he went only two at-bats between long balls before hitting his 67th at 4:12 p.m. CDT. On the way to the dugout, he saluted to the Cardinals' owners, as has become his custom, then made a curtain call to thunderous applause.

There was only a one at-bat gap before No. 68, which came at 5:38 p.m. CDT.

The fan who caught No. 67

Mark McGwire waves to the cheering crowd after hitting his 67th home run of the season, in the fourth inning against Montreal Expos pitcher Dustin Hermanson, at Busch Stadium in St. Louis, September 26. (AP/Wide World Photos—James A. Finley)

said he'd give it to the Hall of Fame. Doug Singer, 30, of Dallas flew to St. Louis with a buddy, who bought tickets for the weekend series three months ago.

Heath Wiseman, 25, a veterinary student at Illinois State, caught No. 68. Wiseman, who is from Ames, Iowa, is in town for a bachelor party and he and a group of friends said they planned to "exploit" the ball.

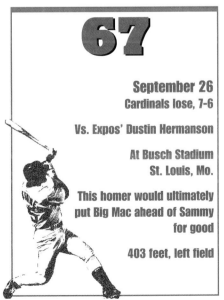

67

September 26
Cardinals lose, 7-6

Vs. Expos' Dustin Hermanson

**At Busch Stadium
St. Louis, Mo.**

This homer would ultimately put Big Mac ahead of Sammy for good

403 feet, left field

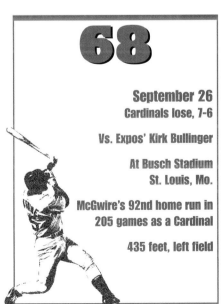

68

September 26
Cardinals lose, 7-6

Vs. Expos' Kirk Bullinger

**At Busch Stadium
St. Louis, Mo.**

McGwire's 92nd home run in 205 games as a Cardinal

435 feet, left field

THE KING OF SWING

By R.B. FALLSTROM
AP Sports Writer

"Swing and ... . Get up, baby! Get up, get up, get up. Home run! He's done it again! Seventy home runs! Take a ride on that for history! They'll be shooting at that one for years and years!
—Cardinals broadcaster Mike Shannon, calling Big Mac's 70th home run

ST. LOUIS (AP)—With his last swing of the season, Mark McGwire gave baseball its new magic number—70. And even he knows he might not be around to see this record broken.

The St. Louis slugger wrapped up his record-smashing season as mightily as he started it, hitting his 69th and 70th homers in a fitting finale to a year that began with a grand slam on opening day.

Like No. 62 that broke Roger Maris' record, McGwire's 70th and final home run of the season was a line shot over the left-field wall on a first-pitch fastball. It came at 3:19 p.m. CDT on a humid, sun-splashed day off Montreal's Carl Pavano in the seventh inning.

"This is a season I will never, ever forget, and I hope everybody in baseball never forgets," an emotional McGwire told the cheering crowd at Busch Stadium after the game.

It will be hard to forget the home run derby that riveted all of baseball and much of America in 1998, as McGwire and his genial rival, the Cubs' Sammy Sosa, chased Maris' 37-year-old record.

Slammin' Sammy, with 66 home runs, went 2-for-5 with no homers as the Cubs lost to Houston 4-3 in 11 innings, but his season is not done. The Cubs face San Francisco at Wrigley Field on Monday night in a one-game tiebreaker for the wild-card spot—a game in which Sosa's stats will count.

But with his five homers on the final weekend, Big Mac put an emphatic conclusion to his season and left many wondering whether his record will ever be surpassed.

"I think it will stand for a while. I know how grueling it is to do what I've done this year," he said. "Will it be broken someday? It could be. Will I be alive? Possibly. But if I'm not playing, I'll definitely be there."

McGwire's 69th homer came in the third inning off rookie Mike

Thurman on a 1-1 fastball and went 377 feet into the left-field seats at 2:10 p.m. After stomping on home plate, McGwire took a few slow steps, then made several salutes to the sellout crowd. The fans who had stood well before his at-bat demanded—and got—two curtain calls.

Kerry Woodson, a 22-year-old body-shop worker from Maryland Heights, Mo., wound up with the ball.

"It's a dream come true," said Woodson. "I hope he doesn't hit anymore today."

He didn't get his wish, as McGwire connected off Pavano (6-9) with two outs and two runners on base to send the Cardinals to a 6-3 win.

"Every time the replay is shown, I'm not going to turn the TV off," Pavano said. "I hope he hits 75 next year so people will forget I gave up No. 70."

McGwire said No. 70 felt almost like No. 62, the homer that broke Maris' record on Sept. 8, with the crowd at fever pitch and Expos infielders shaking his hand as he rounded the bases.

"What can I say?" McGwire said. "I'm speechless."

The second home run ball landed in a party box and was snared by Phil Ozersky, 26, of Olivette, Mo. He said he didn't know what he'd do with the ball, which has a standing $1 million offer from collectors.

"It's stranger than fiction, what this man has done," Cardinals manager Tony La Russa said about McGwire's accomplishments.

Expos manager Felipe Alou told his young pitchers to challenge McGwire.

"I left it up to God and the kid on the mound," Alou said. "I didn't want to tamper with history. Thank God the season's over, or he would hit 80."

McGwire opened the year with a slam on March 31 against the

Dodgers' Ramon Martinez, then led the home run race all season except when Sosa twice passed him briefly—and then for only 103 minutes in all. Sosa led for 58 minutes on August 19 before McGwire regained went back ahead with his 48th and 49th homers in the same game at Chicago. Sosa led for 45 minutes on Friday when he hit his 66th before McGwire answered.

McGwire drew his NL record 162nd walk, tying Ted Williams (1947 and 1949) for the second-highest total in major league history, on a pitch that nearly beaned him in the fifth.

The distances of Mark McGwire's homers in 1998 totaled 29,598 feet, nearly 400 feet higher than the peak of Mount Everest. His 70 home runs averaged 422.8 feet per blast.

Mark McGwire rounds the bases after hitting his 70th home run of the season in the seventh inning against Montreal pitcher Carl Pavano, Sept. 26. (AP/Wide World Photos—Amy Sancetta)

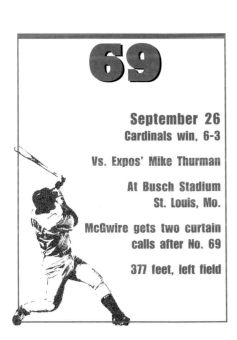

69

September 26
Cardinals win, 6-3

Vs. Expos' Mike Thurman

At Busch Stadium
St. Louis, Mo.

McGwire gets two curtain calls after No. 69

377 feet, left field

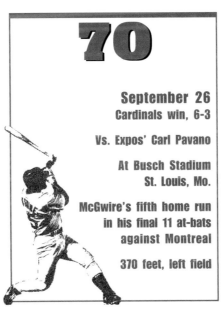

70

September 26
Cardinals win, 6-3

Vs. Expos' Carl Pavano

At Busch Stadium
St. Louis, Mo.

McGwire's fifth home run in his final 11 at-bats against Montreal

370 feet, left field

SAMMY AND THE HURRICANE

By NIKO PRICE
Associated Press Writer

> "Sammy will come back soon, and he will help."
> — Eduardo Torreano, Sammy Sosa's childhood friend

SAN PEDRO DE MACORIS, Dominican Republic (AP)—Christian Vallenilla picked up a wooden stick, then smacked his third home run of the day in the stadium where Sammy Sosa used to play.

"This one's for Sammy," the 11-year-old boy said.

Hurricane Georges nearly destroyed the stadium in Sosa's hometown of San Pedro de Macoris. Light towers twisted to the ground and girders stretched skyward where a roof used to be. In the bleachers, soiled laundry dried.

The outfield wall is gone, and Christian's house, half-flattened by the hurricane, now has a direct view of home plate.

Still, the town that watched Sosa grow up somehow kept up as its favorite slugger tried for the home-run record and a postseason berth.

Sosa's hurricane-ravaged hometown of San Pedro de Macoris celebrated his remarkable season, one that produced 66 home runs.

"We can't ask for any more, because he's done a lot already. He's broken a lot of records," said Arizmendi Nunez, a 22-year-old San Pedro bartender. "I feel proud because now our flag is raised high."

Amid the misery of a place with no power, telephones or running water, hundreds in this baseball-crazed city scrambled to find places to hear Sosa's final regular-season game on radio.

It wasn't easy. The lone TV station broadcasting in the Dominican Republic had a movie about a hurricane on, and without batteries to power their radios, most San Pedro residents didn't catch the game.

Men craned their necks into taxis stopped at street corners for radio updates. Some crowded into sports betting parlors around the city.

Four men listened to the game in a carpentry shop with no roof and one wall blown away. "We're in bad shape. We're in the street, but we're celebrating today," said Lorenzo Mota, 34, an off-duty police agent.

The only place in San Pedro where the game was televised was the Flor y Mar bar, where a group of U.S. and other TV networks covering fan reaction set up a live satellite feed.

Drinking plenty of Presidente beer, the crowd of 100 people jumped up and down and chanted, "Sammy! Sammy!" every time Sosa batted. They cheered when Sosa hit a fly ball, and groaned collectively when it was caught.

"He didn't do bad. He did magnificently well," said Pedro Garcia, a 34-year-old accountant.

Sosa and the Cubs still have at least one more game, a Monday night playoff with San Francisco to decide the National League wild-card. The Giants lost to Colorado 9-8 minutes after the Astros beat Chicago.

The children playing a pickup game in the stadium outfield all lived in houses heavily damaged by Georges. But they still found time to

Fans in Sammy Sosa's home town of San Pedro de Macoris react as their idol goes to bat in the season finale versus Houston. Amid the destruction of Hurricane Georges, which left many with no power, telephones or running water, hundreds of people scrambled to find places to see or hear Sosa's final regular-season game. (AP/Wide World Photos—Jose Luis Magana)

play and to pose for pictures, giving Sosa's trademark two-fingered salute.

"I want to be a great ballplayer just like Sammy Sosa," Christian said. "We play a lot of ball here."

Sosa's seven-bedroom house received little damage—a few broken windows and a toppled yard fence.

His kid brother Carlos, 21, said the Sosa family was thinking about those less fortunate. The storm killed more than 200 Dominicans and made thousands homeless.

"I know what the poor masses are. I was one of the poor masses and I know what it is to have a house one day and the next not have anything," Carlos said.

Sammy, he added, felt the same way and planned to help San Pedro get back on its feet.

"Sammy is one of those people who, if you are happy, then he's happy," Carlos said.

Georges' eye passed over this city about 40 miles east of Santo Domingo, and most homes sustained moderate to severe damage. Three people were killed in town. Fallen trees and power lines littered the muddy streets.

Two doors down from a shopping mall owned by Sosa—Plaza 30-30, named after his first 30-homer, 30-steal season—long lines formed outside a water distribution center. One man siphoned water from a plaza fountain, which has a small statue of Sosa.

Eduardo Torreano, 32, said he used to shine shoes and wash cars with Sosa when they were kids. Torreano, who lost his home to the hurricane, still does.

"We are his people. He hasn't forgotten us," Torreano said of Sosa.

MAKING TIME FOR MATTHEW

By R.B. FALLSTROM
AP Sports Writer

ST. LOUIS (AP)—Mark McGwire is tired of hitting baseballs. Now it's time to hit the beach.

On Monday, that was the destination of the 70-homer man, back in Southern California after carrying the burden of unreal expectations for six months and then achieving something few could have imagined.

"I'm like in awe of myself," McGwire said.

Why not? This year, everybody else in baseball played in his huge shadow.

"He's provided moment after moment after moment after moment," St. Louis Cardinals manager Tony La Russa said. "It's been unbelievable theater."

And now he'll steal some time for himself. Don't look for McGwire to be hawking shaving cream or pickup trucks, or having a book ghost-written, or to be spending time on the banquet circuit.

"He's going to be real hard to find," La Russa said.

McGwire's needs are simple: He wants to spend a lot more time with his 10-year-old son, Matthew, who lives most of the year in California with McGwire's ex-wife. Maybe he'll get to tool around in the 1962 red Corvette which has been sit-ting in his garage since he broke Roger Maris' home run record.

And oh yes, he'll try to work on that pasty complexion.

"I don't have a tan," McGwire said. "So they'll say, 'Who's the guy from the East Coast?'"

Of the numerous endorsement offers he's already received, McGwire said, "Nothing's really turning my crank."

"I won't allow anything to take me away from my winter," he said. "I don't do any personal appearances. If you get caught up into that stuff, the next thing you know it's spring training, and I don't want that to happen."

He's definitely against seeing a movie made about the season.

"The whole country already saw the movie, so why would they want to do one?" McGwire said. "They saw the whole thing happening. That's the real thing, there's no Hollywood get-up."

Since arriving in St. Louis on July 31, 1997, McGwire has had enough attention for an entire career. September was a blur of sell-out crowds standing in anticipation and seldom leaving disappointed.

He scaled a Mount Everest of homers, with their distance this year alone totaling an estimated 29,598 feet. He was an equal-opportunity destroyer, hitting them off 65 pitchers.

His good-natured duel with Sammy Sosa enthralled fans down the stretch. McGwire ended his season four ahead of Sosa.

All this, despite McGwire's strict, almost religious adherence to the strike zone. During one frustrat-

Mark McGwire's Career Statistics (through 1998)

Year, Team	Regular Season					
	AB	R	H	HR	RBI	Avg.
1986, Oakland	53	10	10	3	9	.189
1987, Oakland	557	97	161	49	118	.289
1988, Oakland	550	87	143	32	99	.260
1989, Oakland	490	74	113	33	95	.231
1990, Oakland	523	87	123	39	108	.235
1991, Oakland	483	62	97	22	75	.201
1992, Oakland	467	87	125	42	104	.268
1993, Oakland	84	16	28	9	24	.333
1994, Oakland	135	26	34	9	25	.252
1995, Oakland	317	75	87	39	90	.274
1996, Oakland	423	104	132	52	113	.312
1997, Oakland	366	48	104	34	81	.284
1997, St. Louis	174	38	44	24	42	.253
1998, St. Louis	509	130	152	70	147	.299
Totals	5131	941	1353	457	1130	.264

Mark McGwire tips his helmet to his adoring fans. (AP/Wide World Photos—James A. Finley)

ing stretch, La Russa predicted McGwire would top Babe Ruth's 1923 record of 170 walks by Sept. 1. McGwire ended at 162 walks, one for every game of the season.

McGwire earned every bit of the dollar-a-head bonus the Cardinals gave him for every paying customer past 2.8 million, leading the team to a franchise attendance record of 3,195,021.

And when the pressure was on, he got even better. After Sosa tied him at 66, McGwire hit five homers in his final 11 at-bats.

"I've amazed myself that I've stayed in such a tunnel for so long throughout what I had to deal with as far as the media, the expectations, almost every eye in the country watching," McGwire said.

Led by McGwire, the Cardinals

won 11 of their final 14 games and finished 83-79, 10 wins better than last year but 19 games behind Houston, the NL Central champion.

"What the second half shows is a lot about the 1998 team and a little bit about 1999," La Russa said.

At the top of the offseason shopping list for general manager Walt Jocketty is a proven shortstop (Barry Larkin?) and a No. 1 starter (Andy Benes?). The Cardinals needed a closer, but may have discovered one in Juan Acevedo, who finished the year with 15 saves and 16 consecutive scoreless outings.

Outfielder Brian Jordan and second baseman Delino DeShields both can be free agents, and both may leave. Jordan, despite a strong comeback season from wrist and back injuries with a .316 average, has been

expendable since the Cardinals chose J.D. Drew in the first round of June's amateur draft.

Drew certainly looked ready to step in and be a star in September with a pair of two-homer games, a .417 average and 13 RBIs in only 36 at-bats.

DeShields made $3 million this season and the Cardinals, especially if they can acquire Larkin from Cincinnati, might have to get by with lower-paid talent such as Pat Kelly or Placido Polanco.

Whatever the Cardinals do, they know McGwire wants to return to the postseason for the first time since 1992 with Oakland.

"Without a doubt, everybody plays this game to get a team to the playoffs and World Series," McGwire said. "Maybe next year."

SEPTEMBER 28

SAMMY-MANIA

By NANCY ARMOUR
AP Sports Writer

CHICAGO (AP)—Forget the home run title. There's more Sammy-mania in store.

Sosa lost the greatest home run derby ever, finishing four behind Mark McGwire with 66. But he helped his Chicago Cubs into the playoffs for the first time since 1989, and that means more to him than any individual title.

"I never thought this would happen to me. I'm never going to forget it," said Sosa, who was 2-for-4 in tonight's 5-3 victory over the San Francisco Giants in the NL wild-card tiebreaker.

After running into the locker room to get his wild-card champions T-shirt, Sosa went back on to the field to party with his teammates and adoring fans.

Who needs a home run title when you're on your way to the playoffs?

"We've played all these games and now we get to open the champagne," a drenched Sosa said. "It's been unbelievable. Tonight, I forgot about the home run. I just wanted to win."

The Cubs will play the Atlanta Braves in the first round, beginning Wednesday in Atlanta.

"Chicago Cubs fans are the best in the world!" he said. "This is for you."

Sosa poured champagne on anyone in sight as he headed back to the field, and he and teammate Mark Grace—the only Cub left from 1989—exchanged a big hug.

"I'm glad Sammy gets a chance to play in the postseason. He's been pretty much like me as far as the lean years here," Grace said. "Now he gets a chance to show his talents worldwide, in front of a big audience. Without Sammy, we wouldn't be where we are."

It's been one big party all summer long for Sosa. His teammates caught the fever first as he hit 20 home runs in June. The city of Chicago was swept up soon after.

The whole city of Chicago has had a bad case of Sosa fever this summer, including Michael Jordan. Chicago's other favorite athlete showed up to throw out the first pitch wearing a Cubs jacket and Sosa's No. 21 jersey.

Sosa laughed as Jordan honored him with his own, chest-thumping, finger-kissing salute. Then Sosa hunkered down behind home plate as Jordan, who played minor league baseball for a season during his brief retirement from basketball, wound up. But Jordan's throw sailed far above Sosa's head, and Sosa had to run back to grab the ball.

Jordan walked off the mound laughing as he greeted Sosa with a hug. The two, who've become friends during Sosa's spectacular season, walked off the field arm in arm.

McGwire's five home runs in his last three games gave him the home run title. But Sosa said all season he was chasing the playoffs, and if you ever doubted what was more important, you weren't listening.

"I've been saying all year that he's 'The Man,'" Sosa said again Sunday. "(But) Mark McGwire is going to go home ... and maybe go to the beach. And I'm going to play."

The Chicago fans still held out hope Sosa might catch McGwire. One fan posted a sign along the first-base line reading, "Hey Sammy! Gimme 5!"

"I got 66 home runs," Sosa said. "It's too much for me."

Sosa fell short in his first at-bat, grounding into a double play on check swing to end the first inning.

"I cannot go out there and think about hitting home runs," said Sosa, who didn't talk before tonight's game. "I have to get base hits."

Who'd have thought in spring training—in May, even—that Sosa would have this kind of year? Sure, he had 30-homer seasons the past few years, but this, this has been, to use one of Sosa's favorite words, unbelievable.

"They're both pretty humble

Sammy Sosa's Career Statistics (through 1998)						
Regular Season						
Year, Team	AB	R	H	HR	RBI	Avg.
1989, Texas	84	8	20	1	3	.238
1989, Chicago-A	99	19	27	3	10	.273
1990, Chicago-A	532	72	124	15	70	.233
1991, Chicago-A	316	39	64	10	33	.203
1992, Chicago-N	262	41	68	8	25	.260
1993, Chicago-N	598	92	156	33	93	.261
1994, Chicago-N	426	59	128	25	70	.300
1995, Chicago-N	564	89	151	36	119	.268
1996, Chicago-N	498	84	136	40	100	.273
1997, Chicago-N	642	90	161	36	119	.251
1998, Chicago-N	643	134	198	66	158	.308
Totals	4664	727	1233	273	800	.264

about what has happened," said Gary Gaetti, who started the season with the Cardinals and finished with the Cubs. "It doesn't even look right. It doesn't look right at all for one guy to have those numbers."

When the year began, the money was on McGwire and Ken Griffey Jr. to challenge Roger Maris' season record of 61 homers. Sosa, who trailed McGwire 24-9 in late May, wasn't even on the radar.

Then came June 1. Sosa hit two homers off the Florida Marlins, and he was off on a binge. By the end of the month, he'd hit 20 home runs and the chase for Maris was a three-man race.

Since then, it's been all Sammy, all the time. An entire city thrills to see his little home run hop, and his teammates are constantly amazed.

Even manager Jim Riggleman, who's been asked hundreds of times what Sosa has meant to the Cubs, can only shake his head.

"You can't hardly put it into words. It's just been so unbelievable what he's done," Riggleman said. "He's been huge for the city, for the organization, for his teammates. It's just been an unbelievable story, the '98 season, with Sammy Sosa leading the way."

And nobody's enjoyed it more than Sosa. While McGwire occasionally chafed under the glare of the spotlight, Sosa would ask reporters why they didn't have more questions for him.

"I'll have to say I had a good year," he said. "The appreciation from everybody makes me satisfied. As a human being, I'm very happy."

But Sosa's done more than just hit homers. His 158 RBIs led the majors and fourth-best in NL history. His 416 total bases also led the majors, as did his 133 runs scored. After starting the season having never hit a grand slam, he's now hit three.

Sammy Sosa passes out Dominican cigars in the Cubs lockerroom after Chicago's playoff victory over San Francisco. (AP/Wide World Photos—Mike Fisher)

If all of that doesn't add up to an MVP year, Riggleman doesn't know what does.

"The MVP award is going to be the icing on the cake for him, a statement of what he's really done," Riggleman said. "In a year that a man hit 70 home runs, Sammy Sosa is going to win the MVP. That in itself has to be one of the biggest statements anyone can ever make

about how great a year somebody had."

And now Sosa finally gets to see what it's like to play in October. Just hearing the word playoffs brings a smile to his face, prompting him to repeat his favorite line one more time.

"What a great country, America," he said. "Baseball been very, very good to me."

MAJOR LEAGUE BASEBALL'S CAREER HOME RUN LEADERS

(through 1998)

1.	Hank Aaron	755
2.	Babe Ruth	714
3.	Willie Mays	660
4.	Frank Robinson	586
5.	Harmon Killebrew	573
6.	Reggie Jackson	563
7.	Mike Schmidt	548
8.	Mickey Mantle	536
9.	Jimmie Foxx	534
10.	Willie McCovey	521
	Ted Williams	521
12.	Ernie Banks	512
	Eddie Mathews	512
14.	Mel Ott	511
15.	Eddie Murray	504
16.	Lou Gehrig	493
17.	Stan Musial	475
	Willie Stargell	475
19.	Dave Winfield	465
20.	MARK McGWIRE	457
21.	Carl Yastrzemski	452
22.	Dave Kingman	442
23.	Andre Dawson	438
24.	Billy Williams	426
25.	Darrell Evans	414
26.	Barry Bonds	411
27.	Duke Snider	407

MAJOR LEAGUE BASEBALL'S SINGLE-SEASON HOME RUN LEADERS

(through 1998)

70 — MARK McGWIRE, ST. LOUIS CARDINALS, 1998
66 — SAMMY SOSA, CHICAGO CUBS, 1998
61 — Roger Maris, New York Yankees, 1961
60 — Babe Ruth, New York Yankees, 1927
59 — Babe Ruth, New York Yankees, 1921
58 — Jimmie Foxx, Philadelphia Athletics, 1932
58 — Hank Greenberg, Detroit Tigers, 1938
58 — Mark McGwire, Oakland Athletics and
       St. Louis Cardinals, 1997
56 — Hack Wilson, Chicago Cubs, 1930
56 — KEN GRIFFEY JR., SEATTLE MARINERS, 1998
56 — Ken Griffey Jr., Seattle Mariners, 1997
54 — Babe Ruth, New York Yankees, 1920
54 — Babe Ruth, New York Yankees, 1928
54 — Ralph Kiner, Pittsburgh Pirates, 1949
54 — Mickey Mantle, New York Yankees, 1961
52 — Mickey Mantle, New York Yankees, 1956
52 — Willie Mays, San Francisco Giants, 1965
52 — George Foster, Cincinnati Reds, 1977
52 — Mark McGwire, Oakland Athletics, 1996
51 — Ralph Kiner, Pittsburgh Pirates, 1947
51 — Johnny Mize, New York Giants, 1947
51 — Willie Mays, New York Giants, 1955
51 — Cecil Fielder, Detroit Tigers, 1990
50 — Jimmie Foxx, Boston Red Sox, 1938
50 — Albert Belle, Cleveland Indians, 1995
50 — Brady Anderson, Baltimore Orioles, 1996
50 — GREG VAUGHN, SAN DIEGO PADRES, 1998

Mark McGwire—single-season home run leader (AP/ Wide World Photos—Eric Draper)

Sammy Sosa and Mark McGwire (AP/Wide World Photos—Eric Draper)